The Book of
SEATON

Celebrating a Devon Seaside Town

TED GOSLING

HALSGROVE

First published in Great Britain in 2002

DEDICATED TO THE LATE NORMAN WHINFREY

**His knowledge of the Romans and early primitive man was the
inspiration for this book. His lectures on archaeology for the Axe
Valley Heritage Association always filled the hall to overflowing.**

Frontispiece photograph: *Landing passengers at Seaton, c.1904. The pleasure steamer,* Victoria,
*conveyed passengers to Bournemouth and Weymouth from Torquay, calling on its way at Sidmouth,
Seaton and Lyme Regis. Although these towns had no pier, passengers got ashore via a small bridge
thrown out to the beach from the boat.*

British Library Cataloguing-in-Publication Data
A CIP record for this title is available from the British Library

ISBN 1 84114 192 5

HALSGROVE

Halsgrove House
Lower Moor Way
Tiverton, Devon EX16 6SS
Tel: 01884 243242
Fax: 01884 243325
email: sales@halsgrove.com
website: www.halsgrove.com

Printed and bound by
Bookcraft Ltd, Midsomer Norton

*Whilst every care has been taken to ensure the accuracy of the
information contained in this book, the author disclaims responsibility
for any mistakes which may have inadvertently been included.*

CONTENTS

ACKNOWLEDGEMENTS

I am grateful to the many people who have contributed material for this book. Particular thanks must go to Heather Sanham, without whose help the book would not have been possible. I am grateful to my wife, Carol, for her encouragement and assistance, and to Naomi Cudmore from Halsgrove who gave invaluable help in producing this book.

The photographs all come from the E.S. Gosling Collection, now in the care of Seaton Museum.

Many books, newspapers and organisations were consulted – too many to mention – but the following were a mine of information:

Pulmans Weekly News
Seaton Tramway
Pulmans Book of the Axe
Seaton and District by E.J. Burnham
Express and Echo
The Axe Estuary by Margaret Parkinson, MA
The Honeyditches Roman Villa by Henrietta Miles
Roman Seaton and the Axe by Bob Silvester
The Papers of the late Norman Whinfrey
Devon County Council
East Devon District Council
Exeter Museum
John Allen
Roy Chapple
Axe Valley Heritage Museum
The Papers of the late Eileen Gosney
The Towns of Roman Britain by John Wacher, BA, Seaby Ltd.

The Burrow Munp looking toward the East Walk with the coffee tavern seen on the right, c.1886.

Chapter 1

THE INHERITORS

It is always difficult to decide at what point to launch into the stream of human history. The concern of the archaeologist in any region is with change and succession, with the coming and going of people, the development of tools, weapons and ornaments, the variation in pottery making and design, house or tomb building, and with the growth or decline of settlement areas. There are no fixed points at which to begin or end in the flow of time.

The arbitrary point which I have selected is the arrival from western France of a people with a Neolithic (New Stone Age) culture around 4,000BC. This is, necessarily, just a brief summary and a generalisation.

It is important to emphasise how extremely slow any change was in pre-history. People talk of the Bronze-Age 'revolution' and in terms such as this. There was no such thing. One age merged slowly into another. Stone was used alongside bronze, and both alongside iron.

Another word overused is 'invasion'. The new cultures in Britain are usually ascribed to invasion. But it should not be thought that these were dramatic or like those of the Romans, Anglo-Saxons, Danes or Normans. Some were mere trickles or intrusions. Many new objects or customs were the result of the radiation of ideas, the interchange between communities, and the result of increasing wealth and power on the part of native leaders, rather than the replacement of those leaders by others from abroad. Cultured contact is often more important than invasion; so is continuity of local development.

The first farmers arrived from the Continent by 4,000BC. Bronze-Age and Iron-Age boats came in numbers from the Humber and its tributaries with a prehistoric 'boat yard' at Ferriby. The first boats were of skin with wooden frames (the coracle and curragh being descended from these), or were dug out from logs. Curraghs, in particular, are capable of carrying about three tons of cargo, crew and passengers. With eight to nine humans, such a boat would carry three or four cattle or 15 pigs, or 25 sheep or goats. They could only be carried if tied so it would be difficult to feed and water them. Journeys had to be short and the south and south-west of Britain were the first areas to be settled. However, radio-carbon dates suggest that a very wide area of Britain and Ireland were settled at the same time, perhaps due to coastal movement.

These first farmers introduced the basis for our civilisation. Their origins seem to have been in the area of the Iranian plateau and the Turkish crescent – the land from Iran and Iraq to Syria and Asia Minor and on through Palestine to Egypt. It is significant that all these areas include rivers which flooded regularly and covered the land with fertile silt. Farmers could settle down on land which was permanently fertile, instead of moving from place to place as the ground became exhausted. Crop growing and stock raising were greatly developed and supported large populations; gradually urban centres arose where goods could be exchanged and mutual protection was much easier. Town life was the direct outcome. Sites such as Jericho date back to the early-eighth millennium BC, with reservoirs, temples and market-places.

At this time in Britain we were just moving out of the last Ice Age. The sea was rising but we were still part of mainland Europe. We were on the extreme edge of civilisation and it took around 5,000 years for the culture from the Middle East to reach Britain with the first farmers. We were by then an island. Families began to land on the south and south-west coasts late in the fifth millennium, say 4,300–4,000BC, with a few belongings, seeds and animals. Those in the south worked up the rivers of Kent, Sussex and Hampshire to the chalk hills and downs not far from the sea.

There were the three main routes across Europe:

1st – *The Mediterranean coast to Iberia and round and across France to south-west Britain.*

2nd – *Northwards from Greece to the Danube Valley and across central and northern France to southern England.*

3rd – *Through northern Europe to eastern England.*

The aboriginal Mesolithic people gradually adopted elements of the new way of life and created secondary Neolithic culture. I am not suggesting that people came to Britain from Syria but, rather like a train shunting, the pressures and ideas moved westwards. Collective burials in long barrows and new types of stone tombs were introduced from western Europe. There is some evidence, provided by carbon dating, that the distinctive group of Neolithic people who settled in south-west England were probably the first of the southern group to arrive. Their settlements range from Carn Brea near Camborne in Cornwall to Maiden Castle in Dorset. The Maiden Castle which you see today is a much later Iron-Age construction. The most important site is the causewayed camp at Hembury, which also shows later alteration and occupation. From Hembury came the pottery which differentiates south-western people from those mentioned earlier, who became the Windmill Hill culture.

Our newcomers were still users of implements made of stone, wood, antler and bone. They were experienced in forest clearance and had developed a characteristic stone axe, the efficiency of which was increased by polishing. With the aid of these axes, by ring-barking and by burning, cultivation patches could be cut out of the forests and the grazing livestock then kept the ground clear.

In this area these people are known only from their settlements and chance finds. Their physical appearance can be established from the skeletons of their related contemporaries, inhumed under long barrows in southern England. They were of small stature, lightly boned and neatly built, with well-fashioned – almost delicate – hands and feet, indicating good powers of movement and skill. They had long, thin faces.

In this area the newcomers found the indigenous Mesolithic inhabitants were few and limited to the coasts and open moors.

By 3,000BC there is evidence of long-distance trade. Axes and pottery crafted from Cornish materials were found at Hembury. Tools made of flint from Beer Head were widely distributed. Even axes made from the stone of Great Langdale in Cumbria have been found in the South West. Arrowheads were leaf-shaped and some, now called 'tranchets', were shot with the broad blade of one side forward.

The Neolithic period extended to about 1,700BC but stone tools were used very much later. The obvious remains scattered over the whole of the South West were the tombs and the causewayed camps. The development of tomb buildings in the South West is a phenomenon common to the western seaboards of Britain and Ireland in middle- and late-Neolithic times. It originated in movements of people from Spain, Portugal and the south of France, up the Atlantic coast of Brittany and over to our south-west and Irish-Sea coasts.

In the late-Neolithic period, the characteristic structures were henges and stone circles, a henge being an area enclosed by a bank and internal ditch. They are normally dated to the end of the third millennium BC and about 80 are known in Britain, where there are more than 900 stone circles. All before 2,000–1,700BC then our country was witness to the arrival of farmers with seed and animals, some forest clearance, skill and ability, veneration of the dead – or perhaps the dynastic dead – the ability to organise major constructions like Stonehenge (phase one), a considerable use of seaworthy boats and long-distance trade.

The last major incursion of settlers for over 1,000 years took place somewhere between 2,400 and 2,000BC. They are known as the Beaker people because they introduced a characteristic drinking vessel. But variations in these suggest that seven major groups came here. The first arrivals were two groups from the Rhine delta, in about 2,400BC.

The second wave was of five groups from the Middle Rhine (the area of Mainz and Coblenz), the northern Rhine area and from the coastal area from the Rhine delta to Denmark, and finally from north Holland – the area around Welure. They brought a knowledge of working with copper, but also imported tools, weapons and ornaments from Europe. Burials were single, in round barrows. Very soon full tin bronze replaced copper and burials included beakers, bronze daggers, barbed and tanged flint arrowheads, archers' wristguards or bracers made of bone, battleaxes (the standard weapon used across Europe at this time), bracelets of bronze and beads in jet, shale and amber. Methods of burial varied between the groups. Some are crouched or contracted inhumations with the body in a pit, some are cremations with the ashes under a pile of stones or within a cist and covered by the barrow.

The full early-Bronze Age dawned when all the preceding cultures had settled down and generated their own new culture, which had three (perhaps four) regional variations. Very few houses of this period have been identified because the people, although pastoral, were still somewhat nomadic; perhaps like the North American Indians; their houses were wood and skin structures (remember the boats?) and they left no traces of remains. Only ten sites in Britain have produced evidence of structures which might be domestic and they follow no pattern.

From about 2,100BC Wessex saw the rise and development of a rich and powerful mercantile aristocracy which traded as far as Greece, Iberia and the Baltic. They seem to have reached a peak about 1,600BC when Stonehenge was again remodelled and the Aegean daggers carved into its stones. Silbury is another of the astonishing constructions.

From about 1,500–1,000BC life in Britain seems to have settled down to an uneventful, and not very exciting, aftermath of the earlier cultures.

From about 1,000BC (the late-Bronze Age), there are two important features. First, the obviously great increase in the availability of metal tools and metal working techniques, and second, the introduction of the plough, which enabled more land to be cultivated, more food to be grown and more people to be fed.

The first phase, 1,000–800BC, was also marked by the advent of foreign types of metalware, probably brought in by traders or made by travelling smiths. The new sword with a leaf-shaped blade was a great improvement; socketed axes meant better wood-working, and riveted spearheads also arrived.

The second phase, 800–750BC, saw the arrival of colonists from Holland and the Rhineland. They were intensive farmers and had a plough which could be drawn by oxen. They cremated their dead and buried them in urnfields, although there were some single burials under barrows.

The third phase of 100 years to 650BC overlaps the earlier part of the Iron Age on the Continent (the Hallstatt Culture) and objects of iron, swords, razors, etc., found their way to Britain.

Three waves of settlers, equipped with iron tools and weapons, then arrived:

Iron Age A   700–400BC *(Hallstatt Culture)*
Iron Age B   400–150BC *(La Tene Culture)*
Iron Age C   150BC–AD43 *(The Elgaue)*

The Hallstatt Culture was essentially a continuation of the late-Bronze Age but with iron implements. (This is, of course, a simplification.)

The La Tene Culture reflected Greek influences with superior social organisation and a characteristic art style.

The Hallstatt people (mainly Beakes) came from Wessex and landed in Yorkshire; they lived in farms and villages, grew corn extensively, parched it so that it would keep and stored it in pits lined with matting. They had threshing floors, frames for drying corn and hay, and granary platforms for seeds. They kept cattle, sheep and pigs. They built hillforts all over their settlement areas.

With their arrival, we at last begin to emerge from the long bewildering succession of nameless peoples into the dawn of history, with references to individual tribes by the classical writers. States of a recognisable type were set up with dynasties of kings. The language was Celtic – an ancestor of Welsh – although Indo-European tongues may have been spoken in Britain, perhaps ever since Beaker times.

Members of the Axe Valley Heritage Association are seen gathered around Norman Whinfrey, who was giving a talk on Blackbury Castle when the association paid a visit to the site in 1987. The enclosure is of Iron-Age date, not later than 200BC. It is roughly oval, or perhaps a D-shape, with the bowed side to the south, on which there is the only original entrance, roughly central. It is defended by a single bank and ditch. It should not really be called a 'castle', since this is misleading and, in any event, 'bury' means the strong or fortified place. Ted Gosling Collection.

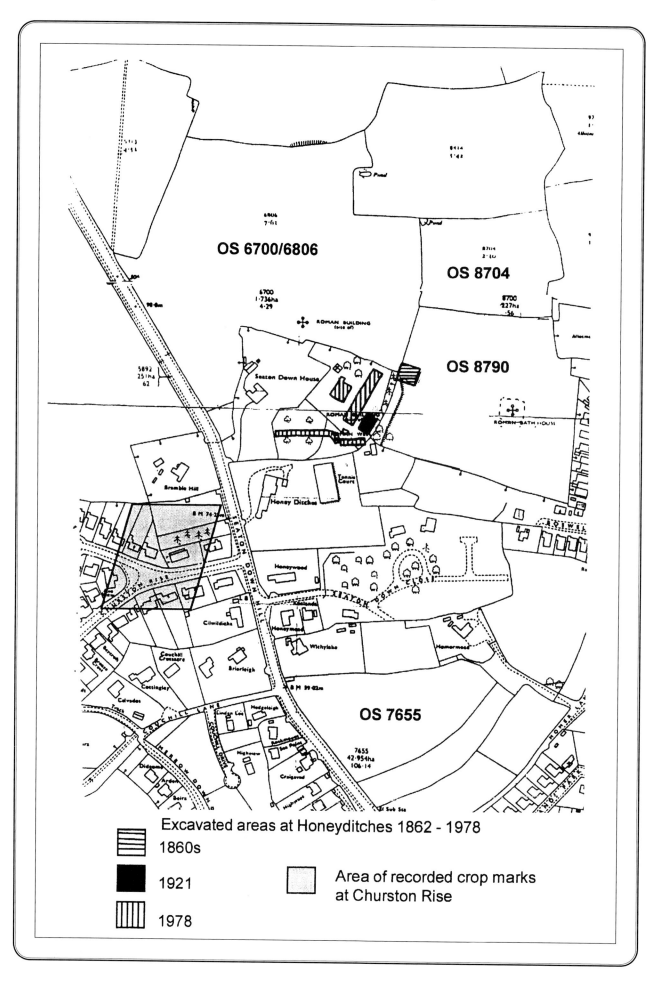

OS 6700/6806

OS 8704

OS 8790

OS 7655

Excavated areas at Honeyditches 1862 - 1978

1860s

1921

1978

Area of recorded crop marks
at Churston Rise

Chapter 2

ROMAN SEATON

For nearly four centuries, with the might of their armies and the strength of their administration, the Romans occupied Britain. They brought with them the graces of their civilisation and succeeded in overcoming an environment they found so sadly lacking in culture and comfort, traces of which can be found in the Roman site at Seaton, set on the gentle western slopes above the Axe estuary.

Honeyditches, which lies on the edge of modern Seaton, is one of the most important and puzzling Roman sites in Devon. This favoured spot had been occupied by successive farming communities between around 4000BC and AD50 – by Neolithic, Bronze-Age and Iron-Age people. Just before the Roman Conquest of Devon there was an open farming settlement here, whose circular houses were of timber with thatched roofs. This continued in use long into the Roman period. Around AD150–250 this community was replaced by at least three ranges of long stone buildings which included a small bathhouse, with fine mosaic in at least one room.

The earliest recorded discovery at Honeyditches was in 1859, when buried stone foundations were exposed during hedge removal, but Seaton had long been considered by early topographers to have been the site of the Roman Moridunum of Antonius. In Camden's *Britannia*, published in 1623, we read:

Seaton, formerly a fine harbour but now so choked with sand heap'd before the mouth of them by the ebbing and flowing of the sea, that the benefit is almost quite lost. Here at Seaton the inhabitants endeavoured to cut out a harbour and proceed under the Great Seal for that purpose but now there remains no foundation of that work [Camden is here referring to Collaton Haven, the vast enterprise that never took place]. *That is the Moridunum of Antonius which is situated between Isca and Durnovaria (if the book be not faulty)... I should conjecture both from the Distance and the Signification of the Name. For Moridunum is the same in Britain that Seaton is in English, namely a town upon a hill by the sea!* [Camden was quoting from the *Antoline Itinerary* of about AD200–300.]

The antiquary William Stukeley spent a considerable time in this neighbourhood during the summers of 1723 and 1724 and in his *Itineracium Curiosum* writes:

About half a mile from the harbour, upon higher ground on the western side, is a castle in a pasture but formerly tilled called Honey Ditches. Tis noted about [has a ditch] *and perhaps walled for they dig up much squared stone there.*

From 1862 onwards a series of excavations was carried out by the lord of the manor, Sir Walter Trevelyan. Work was concentrated in the field now known as AS8790. The well-known Peter Orlando Hutchinson from Sidmouth took an active part in these investigations and the results are briefly summarised in his paper published in the *Transactions of the Devonshire Association, Volume 2* (1868), pages 379–81. P.O. Hutchinson's full report, with a sketch of the site, is now in the possession of the Sidmouth Museum.

The nineteenth-century explorations located the site of a Roman bathhouse with a hypocaust, quantities of roofing tiles of lias from Dorset and fragments of tessellated pavement. The most important of all the finds was a tile of the 2nd Augustine Legion which built the Roman fortress of Exeter. This is now in Taunton Museum but some have expressed doubt about this tile and suggested it might have come from another site.

At Trevelyan's dig a considerable amount of medieval pottery was found, along with medieval tiles and heavy slates with peg holes. In Sir Walter's diary he states that all the stone flints had been removed to build the new cottages south of the old school, now Seaton Women's Institute room in Harepath Road.

Sir Walter Trevelyan, ever the romantic, got Sam Good, a local builder, to place the letters 'Moridunum' over the south side of the remains of the Napoleonic shore fort. This had been cut away in 1836 to make way for a road to the harbour. The letters were taken down in 1937 when the toilets were built. (In all, four stone shore forts have stood south of Fossway Court.)

In 1912 Major-General H.B.H. Wright, CB, CMG, built a new house on Seaton Down in a field known as Lomans Boswell, and named the property Seaton Down House. In the autumn of 1920 a plantation of fruit trees was put in on the easternmost and lower part of his ground. When the first trees were planted, large stones were found which obviously had not

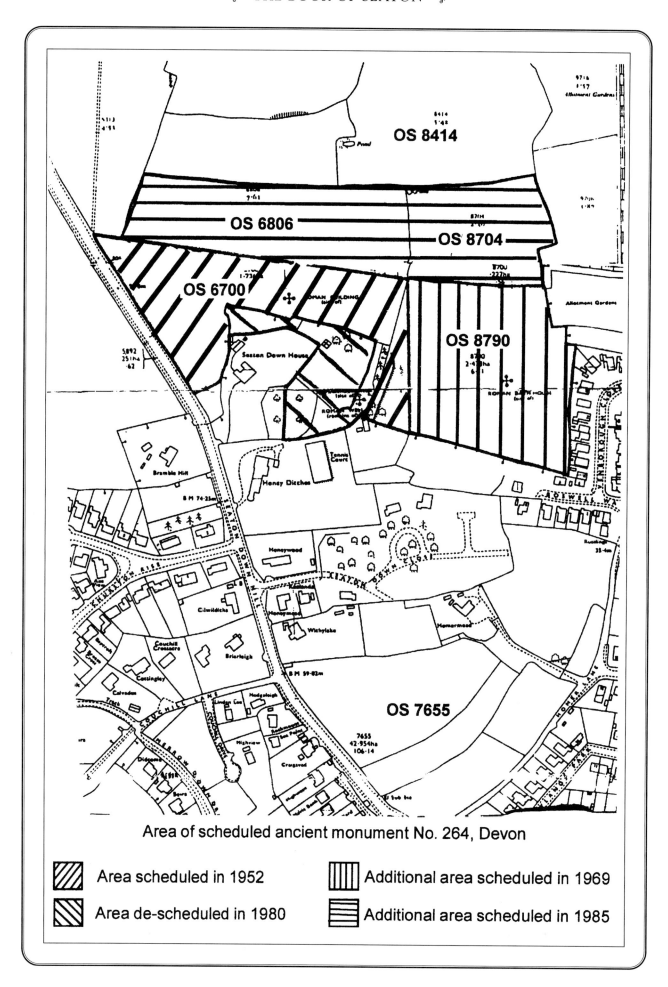

Area of scheduled ancient monument No. 264, Devon

Honeyditches Villa. The plaster-lined bath and part of the Hot Room, looking north.
Courtesy of Seaton Museum.

*Honeyditches Villa. Beer-stone ashlar quions and chert walling on the outside of the bath
in the Hot Room, looking west.* Courtesy of Seaton Museum.

The excavation of the bath house in 1969: its walls stood about a metre or more high. The pillars visible within the building supported the raised floor of the Hot Room. Courtesy of Seaton Museum.

A detail of the excavation of the Roman bath house: the semi-circular bath beside the Hot Room with its plastered floors and walls still preserved. Courtesy of Seaton Museum.

been placed by nature. Work proceeded and on Good Friday 1921, at a depth of 2ft 6in to 3ft, a pavement made of small square stone blocks was uncovered.

Further careful work revealed that this was the outer border of a more elaborate tessellated pavement made of smaller blocks about half an inch square and coloured. Major-General Wright called in Professor Claydon, who lived at The Pines, Beer. He was the principal of the College of the South West, now Exeter University, and dated the finds to AD200. Further excavations led to the uncovering of two stone-built rooms with fragments of Roman mosaic and traces of a hypocaust heating system. In Rome the hypocaust heating system was mostly restricted to the heating of baths but here, in the cold of a Devon winter, it might have been adopted for heating rooms. A stoke-hole on an outside wall fed a furnace with charcoal from which heat radiated in channels underneath the floors, which were supported by stone or brick pillars. In this case the pillars were of Beer stone. The floor of one of the rooms, sealed a circular well, is also thought to be of Roman date. A brief account of these discoveries was published in the *Transactions of the Devonshire Association, Volume 54* (1922), pages 66–68.

The existence of this important archaeological site had been known for a long time, yet over 30 years were to pass before further excavations took place. With hindsight, an opportunity to provide a heritage centre featuring Roman Seaton was lost to the town. This would have attracted visitors to the area in a way that other places with Roman connections have successfully exploited.

Local historians like A.J. Skinner and Ernest Burnham kept a watching brief but nothing happened until 1960 when members of the Devon Archaeological Exploration Society and the Devonshire Association opened up two trial trenches in the upper part of O.S. 8790. A number of trial trenches revealed layers of heavy slate, as though a building had fallen down. There was also Iron-Age pottery, the remains of a stone drain and a considerable amount of hypocaust tiling – as if it had been piled there during Trevelyan's excavation.

This small investigation was organised by Eileen Gosney. Miss Gosney, the daughter of a local chemist, was a noted local historian who spent her life researching the history of her native town, Seaton. Under her capable direction, the existence of Roman buildings, with finds dating to the second and third centuries AD, were confirmed. A brief note of this work was published in the *Proceedings of the Devon Archaeological Exploration Society, No. 21* (1963), pages 31–32.

In 1969, following a proposal to develop the site, a massive excavation took place. Mrs Henrietta Miles was appointed director of the excavation by the Ministry of Works, now the Department of the Environment.

Initial work by Mrs Sheila Pollard of the Devon Archaeological Society concentrated on the Roman trackway running along the upper edge of O.S. 8790. This was followed by extensive trenching throughout the field, under the direction of Mrs Miles. She recorded a complex sequence of occupation from the first to the fourth centuries AD, with further activity in the medieval period. First-century features included a roundhouse in the prehistoric tradition (which underlay the Roman bathhouse) and at least two farmyard enclosures. The main Roman features were the bathhouse, built in the second or third century, the barn complex overlying an earlier hypocausted building which seems to form part of a range at right angles to the Roman building discovered in 1921, a large enclosure ditch of the third century, and long narrow ranges of timber buildings of uncertain age.

Mrs Sheila Pollard found a considerable stretch of Roman road or trackway leading towards Harepath Hill, the ancient Herepath or war path, the present A3052. Mrs Pollard's excavation report is published in the *Proceedings of the Devon Archaeological Society, Volume 30* (1972), pages 222–26.

Henrietta Miles's report of 'Honey Ditches Roman Villa, Seaton', appeared in *Britannia VI*, published by the Society for Roman Studies. A full report is given of the Roman bath with its pilas (pillars), now in the possession of the Exeter Museum, the hypocaust and the various rooms connected with the bath. Beer stone had been used extensively but there had been much stone robbing at the end of the Roman period and again from the medieval period onwards. Fragmented remains of painted plasterwork were found in the bathhouse. This makes us think it once had an owner of high standing. Mrs Miles also found the remains of a poor twelfth-century cottage superimposed on the bath, with pottery of that period. Immediately below the site of the villa, remains of two long timber buildings and a barn were found, dated AD200, and also the remains of a first-century house.

Summing up the excavation, Mrs Miles states:

Excavation at Honey Ditches has revealed first century AD occupation in the Iron Age tradition, followed by Roman buildings. The buildings include two parallel long timber structures, a large free-standing bathhouse and probably a barn. These buildings, together with a house explored earlier this century (Wright 1922), are interpreted as a villa complex, probably dating from the second to the fourth century AD.

A second programme of rescue excavations was mounted by the Devon Committee for Rescue Archaeology in 1978 as a response to the construction of a new housing development in the grounds of Seaton Down House. The extent of these investigations, which were directed by Mr R.J. Silvester, was limited to the areas of new access roads and a few new house sites. As a result, only a partial picture of

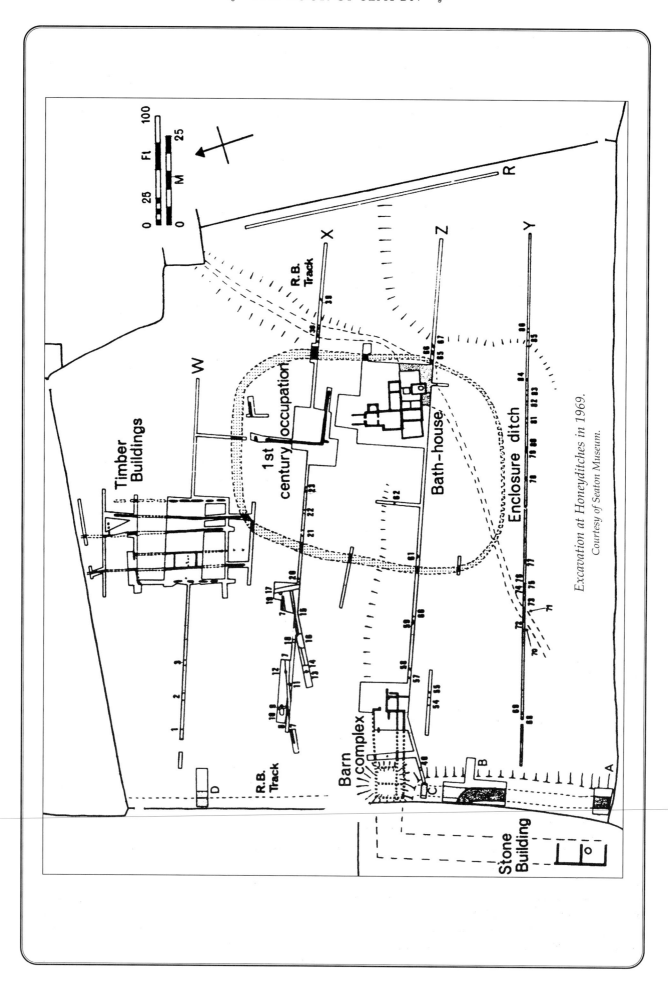

Excavation at Honeyditches in 1969.
Courtesy of Seaton Museum.

archaeological features on this land from O.S. 8790 could be obtained. Mr Silvester's work uncovered evidence of prehistoric activity on this land dating back over 6,000 years, with occupation in the Neolithic, Beaker and Iron-Age periods. A late-Iron-Age farmstead with roundhouses seems to have occupied the site and this gave way to the Roman occupation which extended down into O.S. 8790. Of particular interest was the discovery of further stone Roman buildings to the south-west of the range, uncovered by Major-General Wright in 1921. As part of the landscaping works undertaken during the construction of the new houses in 1978, the area of the range uncovered in 1921 was left undeveloped and protected by dumping topsoil over it to a substantial height.

Mr Silvester's excavation report is published in the *Proceedings of the Devon Archaeological Society, Volume 39* (1981), pages 37–87.

In an attempt to record more details of the extent of buried remains at Honeyditches, the Ancient Monuments Laboratory of English Heritage undertook a geophysical survey in 1984. This work was concentrated in O.S. 8790 with an additional 30-metre square in both O.S. 6700 and O.S. 8704. The survey indicated the existence of additional ditches and structures on the site.

Fresh archaeological work in July 1987 brought about the need to obtain further information on the extent of remains at Honeyditches. This need arose during East Devon District Council's consideration of development proposals, particularly for O.S. 8790 and 8704. Pending more archaeological information, the District Council postponed further decisions on future development in this area.

The various changes to the scheduled area at Honeyditches reflect the way in which our knowledge of the site's archaeology has grown. As it is an Ancient Monument of National Importance scheduled under the Ancient Monuments and Archaeological Areas Act 1979, scheduled monument consent must be obtained from the Secretary of State for any new works affecting the area. Such consent, which may be granted or refused by the Secretary of State on the advice of English Heritage, is additional to any need for planning permission.

Following the discovery of the Roman bathhouse in 1969, there was considerable discussion about preserving the remains for public display. Substantial remains of the bathhouse sub-structure had survived and fragments of glass, wall plaster and other fittings gave an idea of the building's overall construction details. In the end, plans to display the bathhouse did not proceed and the remains were covered over. Fresh excavation would be required to ascertain how these remains have fared over the last 30 years.

Once again an opportunity was lost to promote Roman Seaton to visitors. In my opinion, it was a great shame that the plans to display the bathhouse, with an information centre, did not proceed.

The main phases of occupation may be set out as follows:

Prehistoric settlement
The site is now known to have a settlement history dating back as much as 6,000 years and the discovery of early Neolithic and Beaker material gives it added significance in terms of prehistoric archaeology. A prehistoric farmstead occupied the hillslope in the centuries before the Roman Conquest of AD43 and settlement with roundhouses in the prehistoric tradition continued well into the first century AD. The crop marks in the area of Churston Rise may indicate the site of a late-prehistoric defensive enclosure.

Roman settlement
The Roman occupation at Honeyditches has usually been identified as being that of a Roman villa. The remains excavated to date suggest that the site, with its detached bathhouse, would have formed part of a large rural estate. There is the added possibility that it might even indicate the existence of a small town or coastal settlement at the mouth of the Axe estuary.

More recently, attention has been turned to the evidence of Roman military occupation at Honeyditches. In addition to two finds of Roman military material, the timber buildings in the north of O.S. 8790 are akin to military barrack blocks and it now seems probable that at some stage(s) in its history, the site was given over to Roman military occupation, connected with the use of the Axe estuary as a safe harbour.

Finds from the Honeyditches Site

The excavations described above have produced a large and varied selection of small finds, together with some larger architectural pieces. Finds and records from the 1921 excavation are said to have been destroyed in the Exeter Blitz, but at least one reconstructed section of mosaic and some photographs are known to survive in the Exeter City Museums collection.

Seaton Museum
During the winter of 1998–99 it was felt that to further enhance the Roman display, two panels recording detailed information of Roman Seaton should be commissioned. This job was given to Alan Murray of Murray Design and, at the same time, three showcases were commissioned to display some of the finds from Honeyditches. Three of the Beer-stone hypocaust pillars are also on show.

Chance Finds
Over the years there have been several suggestions of other finds, such as Roman coins and tile fragments, turning up on building sites and other land in

---

Condition and Conservation Status of the Honeyditches site

Condition: The central area of the site now lies on the fringes of the built-up limits of Seaton and parts of the site are already known to lie beneath modern housing developments. O.S. 8790 remains an open pasture field with the partially back-filled spoil heaps of the 1969 bathhouse excavations plainly visible. O.S. 8704 to the north and O.S. 6700 to the north-west are also pasture fields, but otherwise O.S. 8790 is surrounded by modern development. O.S. 8790 and 8704 are in the ownership of East Devon District Council, as is O.S. 8414 to the north of O.S. 8704.

Conservation Status: The Honeyditches site was scheduled as an Ancient Monument of National Importance by the Ministry of Public Buildings and Works in 1952. The Ministry extended the scheduled area in 1969 to include the area of the bathhouse. The scheduled area was slightly reduced by the Department of the Environment in 1980 to take account of the new housing development in the grounds of Seaton Down House. In 1985 the Secretary of State for the Environment extended the scheduled area to include O.S. 8704 and part of O.S. 6700. The site is recorded as Ancient Monument No. 264, Devon.

---

the vicinity of Honeyditches. As far as is known, no systematic record of these chance finds has been kept and the finds themselves have been lost or dispersed privately. They serve as another indication that the archaeological site at Honeyditches is an extensive one.

Over the past ten years, metal-detector users have brought the Roman coins found in the lower Axe Valley to the museum for identification and I have lost count of the tile fragments we have been given.

In Conclusion

The sea and the river dominate the landscape from Seaton Down Hill as they have always done. The Romans would have seen the same green world in the valley that we see today and although much has changed, the outline remains the same.

I often wonder what they thought of this strange land, so green and beautiful in the summer, so lacking the warmth of the Mediterranean sun in the winter. I have read that there was a complete absence of racial feeling in the Roman Empire and intermarriage called for no comment. Did any of them become involved with the local girls to settle down and remain in Seaton?

VESPASIAN
A.D. 69-79

AE SESTERTIUS EMPEROR VESPASIAN COPPER COIN

The son of a tax gatherer Flavius Vespasianus was born at Falcrina in AD 9. Despite coming from a humble origin, his military skill carried him to a series of important positions and he commanded part of the forces which invaded Britain under Claudius.
It was in AD 43 that the emperor Claudius, personally took part in the invasion of Britain to begin the Roman occupation which was to last until the fifth century.
We know that Vespasian was in Devon during this period and the town of Isca (Exeter), which was founded about AD 50, certainly felt his presence.
Vespasian was proclaimed emperor on 1st July AD 69 and proved to be a just and industrious ruler. He died at Reate on 24th June AD 79.

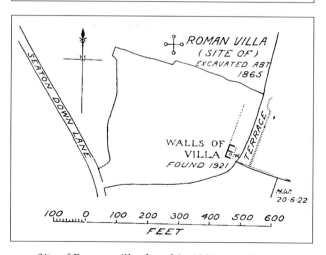

Site of Roman villa, found in 1921, near Seaton.

Tessellated pavement.

To the few scattered people who lived here before the Romans arrived, these newcomers must have cut dashing figures with their feathered plumes in their helmets.

They knew the summer mornings and the sparkle of dew on gossamer, the quietness of moonlight and the greenness of spring. They knew these things and, perhaps, were as joyful as we are about them.

The following paper on Seaton Couchill was written by the late Norman Whinfrey for the Axe Valley Heritage Association in 1989.

In the recently published *Proceedings of the Devon Archaeological Society*, Neil Holbrook, who was in charge of the 1987 Honeyditches excavations, refers to the possibility of a Roman fort on Couchill.

In 1776, William Stukeley wrote of his visit to Seaton:

Half a mile offer, upon higher grounds, on the western side [of the Axe] is a castle in a pasture, but formerly tilled, called Honey Ditches: it is moted about, and perhaps walled; for they dig up much square stone there. The place is an oblong square, containing about three acres: I guess it to have been the garrison of the port.

In 1861, James Davidson further recorded:

At a short distance from Hill Farm other remains, but of a later period, were formerly visible. They were those of an entrenchment, called Hannaditches, about three quarters of a mile from the mouth of the Axe. This earthwork was of a form nearly circular, and if completed would have inclosed an area of about three acres, but it was unfinished on the western side, where the ground rises above its site. The vallum was slight, and seemed to have been hastily thrown up for temporary occupation... All traces of Hannaditches have now disappeared, the vallum having been levelled into the fosse, and the whole brought under the action of the plough.

It is not clear from these accounts whether they refer to the same earthwork and, if so, its precise location. In 1865 the Sidmouth antiquary, P.O. Hutchinson, considered the issue and came to the conclusion that Stukeley's observations did not refer to the Roman buildings partially explored in 1860. In September of 1865 he therefore set out to discover the location of this other site, in the company of his friend Mr Heineken. Initially they examined two fields '100 yards or more' to the west of the stone buildings and found what they took to be fishponds. Thereafter:

... we mounted to the top of Coochill, or Little Coochill, where there are traces of earthworks. A man called Robins, of Seaton, told us he had been employed there about two years ago digging stone, at the top or south end of Field A [Hutchinson's accompanying sketch indicates that this is the field called Long Meadow on the 1839 Tithe Apportionment Map]; that the stone lay in the ground in lines, as if they had been thrown into trenches and covered over; and that they took away scores of cartloads from the position of this hill, commanding as it does the estuary of the Ax [sic], and the whole valley up to Axminster, this looks as if it had been a station...

(Hutchinson MS; DRO MS 36, Vol 2, 1865–71; a shorter version of this account appears in Hutchinson 1868, 380.)

Hutchinson's sketch gives some indication of the largely robbed earthwork: the south-western side was defined by a ridge c.212ft (64.6m) in length, while a measurement of c.220ft (67m) at right angles to the ridge may indicate the extent of stonework recovered from the north-western side. The sketch also allows the precise location of the remains to be fixed at SY23609040, about 5,000m south-west of the Honeyditches buildings, about 1.6km (a mile) from the present mouth of the Axe and roughly 525m from Couchill Farm. It is almost certain, therefore, that it is this site to which both Stukeley and Davidson refer. Stukeley's descriptions probably should be given greater credence as the earthwork was evidently better preserved than when Davidson saw it and Hutchinson's sketch also shows two sides roughly at right angles, rather than a segment of a 'form nearly circular'. As Stukeley and Hutchinson record, the site lies on the eastern side of a small hill 84m above sea level, with commanding views across the mouth of the estuary and up the Axe Valley. The hill is now covered by housing, its southern face having been quarried in the last century by the Seaton Brick Works. Enquiries to households in the area failed to produce any recollections of chance discoveries which may relate to the site.

ARCHAEOLOGICAL OPEN DAY AT THE ROMAN SITE OF HONEYDITCHES, SEATON

SATURDAY 11TH JULY

10.30 AM TO 4.00 PM

Display of finds

Guided tour of site and trial excavations

Roman tile stamp reading L[E]G II AUG (retrograde), from Seaton.

Entrance from Barnard's Hill Lane, off Harepath Road, Seaton

ALL WELCOME   FREE

Organised by
Devon County Council and Exeter City Museums

1987.

Chapter 3

THE FIFTH CENTURY & BEYOND

The Roman occupation of Seaton is confirmed by road systems and by buildings, and recent excavations suggest that it was much more extensive than previously thought.

The Axe estuary was much wider in Roman times since it is almost certain that the marshes on both sides represent estuarine land reclaimed at a later date.

At Axmouth the river was perhaps half a mile wide in Roman times and would have made an important harbour. The Roman coast road from Dorchester to Exeter crossed the Axe at the foot of Boshill to Colyford. We have no evidence of what type of causeway they used to cross what must have been quite deep saltmarsh creeks.

The *Antonine Iter XV* gives the distance from Dorchester to Exeter as 51 miles with an intermediate station, Moridunum, 15 miles from Exeter. The position of Moridunum is unknown and according to the Antonine mileage it should be near Salcombe or near Honiton if on the other route. The Seaton Roman site may represent it, but if so, this would be 20 miles from Exeter.

The letters sent by Honorius to the Civitates of Britain in 410, urging them to look to their own defence, seem to mark the end of Roman Britain. Honorius might have regarded this as a temporary measure to meet a critical situation with the hope that at a future date Britain would be recovered for the Empire. That hope was not fulfilled.

The early-fifth century saw the departure of the Romans. We do not know exactly what happened but we can be fairly sure that life in the Axe Valley must have gone on for a period of 200 years very much as before. Devon was a long way from the east coast, which the Angles and Saxons were attacking, and the Axe Valley remained safe from them until the seventh century. Although there is little archaeological evidence, it seems that by AD600 the Saxons had pushed towards the west and the estuary of the Axe to begin the main assault in the kingdom of Dumnonia.

In 614 the West Saxons defeated the British on Beandun, inflicting heavy casualties upon them. Although the site has not been identified with certainty, there is a very strong case for believing the name to be Bindon in East Devon, which has a commanding position overlooking the estuary of the Axe. Axmouth, during the Saxon occupation of the seventh century, was one of the earliest villages to be founded. There is no reason to suppose that the Axe estuary did not remain much the same at the time of the Romans until well after the Norman Conquest. For the Danish attacks to take place from AD850, a wide open estuary, up which a large fleet could sail, was required. The great Battle of Brunanburgh, fought in the year 957 between King Athelstan and the Danes under Anlaf, is supposed by some to have taken place near Axminster and, upon this doubtful supposition, Seaton is given as the landing place of the Danes.

Leaving the uncertainties of unwritten history, we now come to a period in Seaton with more reliable sources of information. From the charters of Sherborne we learn that Seaton, known then as 'Aut Fleote', was, with some adjoining land, granted in 1005 by King Aethelred to a theign named Eadisge, passing at his death to the Prior of Horton Dorset, to which it was attached at the time the Domesday Book was compiled.

The land conveyed was at least partly in Horton possession by 1086 when the Domesday Book records that the church held half a hide at Fleote (Seaton). The boundaries have been traced by J.B. Davidson in 'Seaton Before the Conquest', *Transaction of the Devonshire Association* (1885), pages 193–98, who found that they outlined the eastern half of Seaton Parish, including a strip of meadowland in the neighbouring parish of Colyton.

Seaton is a comparatively new name for the area, not appearing until 1126 (in the papal privilege of that year). By 1086 the land was gelded at half a hide, a favourable assessment which Davidson suggested was arranged by Ordulf, perhaps as the founder of Horton. By 1086 Horton had also acquired the western half of the parish which included the village of Beer, also gelded at half a hide. In the privilege of 1126, Seaton and Beer are named and the papal text of 1146 includes Beer, Seaton and their salt works, as well as the fisheries of Fleet and Beer.

Horton in Dorset was originally founded as a nunnery, perhaps during the tenth century, but fell into disuse and was refounded as a monastery in the last decades before the Normal Conquest. It was a small house and by 1122 was so poor that it was demoted to a priory and amalgamated with Sherborne which, in turn, was promoted to the status of abbey. Sherborne, with the other ancient monastic houses, continued to dominate the West Country with spectacular buildings and vast estates, encouraging the growth of towns and villages around them.

By 1530 the spiritual value of these monasteries was questioned by many people and the combination of an impecunious king and a ruthless and able minister brought about the rapid fall of these ancient and wealthy institutions.

The Formation Charter of Seaton, AD1005

Fleote was the Saxon name for Seaton. Kemble, *Codex diplomaticus Aevi Saxonici, Vol VI, p152*, No. MCCCI:

XP   In the Name of the Saviour of the World and Redeemer of the human race, Jesus Christ our Lord, who with the Father and Holy Spirit alone holds the everlasting kingdom. I Aethelred by divine ordinance the dutiful King of the English people and of various nations, grant for ever to my one servant called by the name of Eadisge, one house and mansa in the place which in the English tongue is called aet Fleote, for its sufficient price, that is, 100 mancusas of purest gold: so that he may manage always to live of his own in prosperity on this gift and may leave it after him for ever to whomsoever he wishes, by unbreakable indenture. Let the aforesaid land be free from all worldy burden together with everything which is known to belong to the place, as well in great as in the smallest things, fields, pastures, woods, free from military levy and the duty of bridge and castle. And if any person, blown up with tyrannical power, tries to infringe the indenture of this our decree, let him know that he will render an account in terrible scrutiny before Christ and his angels, unless he strives here to amend. These are the boundaries of the aforesaid earth...

In the year of the Lord's Incarnation One thousand and five, the charter of this munificence was drawn up, with the agreement of these witnesses whose names may be seen delineated below.

I Aethelredus, monach of all Britain, have strengthened the gift of my largesse with lineaments of the Holy Cross. I Aethelstanus, son of the same king, have agreed with applause. I Ecgbriht, the prince, was a witness. I Eadmund, the prince, showed my witness. I Eadric, the prince, did not refuse. I Eadwig, the prince, did not draw back. I Eadgar, the prince, did not deny. I Eadweard, the prince, supported. I Aelfgyfu, the Queen, confirmed the truth of the witness. I Aelfricus, Archbishop of the Church of Canterbury, subscribed with the sign of Holy Cross. I Wulfstan, arch ruler of the Church of York signed also. I Aelfheah, the bishop, strengthened it. I Athulf, the bishop, signed also. I Ordbyrht, the bishop, agreed. I Lyfing, the bishop, subscribed. I Godwine, the bishop, did not refuse. I Athelric, the bishop, confirmed. I Alfhelm, the bishop, concluded. I Aelfhun, the bishop, was a witness. I Aelfwold, the bishop, did not deny. I Gemanus, the abbot, etc.

Herein are the Boundaries of the Saxon Estate:

1 –   First from the Sea: at Beer.
2 –   Up to the sheep combe: Beer Street, past the Shepherd's Cottage to Rock Farm.
3 –   South down the Beadle's land: through Barline, up Mare (Manc) Lane, across the cliffs southwards.
4 –   Up to the little valley south of the hidden wood: from Mare Lane, up a trackway to Higher Barn then along the Branscombe – Beer Road to Bovey Fir. At The Barrow there is a trackway leading through a field to the present Bovey House which is in a little valley.
And so on to 18: To the red stream and thence to the River Axe and the sea: From Clapp's Lane to the main Colyford – Seaton Road and thence by Stafford Brook to join the River Axe.

Chapter 4

THE MIDDLE AGES TO THE NINETEENTH CENTURY

The reign of Henry VIII brought a change to Seaton. The Dissolution of the Monasteries meant that the manors of Seaton and Axmouth passed into secular hands. Seaton was sold to a John Frye who in 1557 sold it to John Willoughby. The Willoughby family were of good local standing, having their main residence at Leyhill, Payhembury. They also lived at Combe in Gittisham.

The manor of Seaton included the Marshes, then known as Seaton Common, which was used by local tenants for rough grazing. In 1639 the great-grandson of John Willoughby, another John, saw the advantages of reclaiming the Marshes and commenced proceedings with the common-land tenants to enter into agreements to suspend their rights to the pasture thereon. Unfortunately he soon found that a Mr Wyndham had already obtained a grant from Charles I 'for such lands as are overflown with the ebbing of the sea at Seaton'. The Wyndhams were ardent Royalists and the Willoughbys were on the Parliamentary side, so nothing happened until the Commonwealth, when it was decided that the grant to Mr Wyndham would not hold as the grant from Henry VIII which included all the manorial rights – a bit of political skulduggery here! John Willoughby (dare I call him John Willoughby the fourth) then commenced the reclaiming of Seaton Marshes. A bank was built along the northern boundaries of Seaton and Axmouth (superceded by the tramline) to keep out the fresh water from the river. This was major work and account books show that 300 boatloads of stone from Beer were landed, lines of verticle piles 6ft long were driven deeply into the marsh, and a mention is made of 200 piles of alder from Branscombe.

The work was financed out of the manor rents and repayment of debts. The total amount allocated was £253.13s.7d. and when it was finished the tidal effect was eliminated from one-third of the estuary. A drainage system was necessary and long straight ditches were made, known locally as 'gurts'. After the reclaiming, the salt-marsh area soon became a freshwater marsh and a large number of people were able to graze stock there for various periods, with a weekly charge payable to the manor.

John Willoughby died in 1682 and the manor of Seaton had been inherited as a marriage portion by his eldest daughter Mary when she married George Trevelyan. By the time of her father's death, Mary was a widow and her son John, the second baronet, was only 11 years old. A detailed survey of the estate was carried out and is preserved in the survey book, a foolscap-sized volume, beautifully bound in suede with gold lettering.

A survey of the manor of Seaton was made by Robet Leigh at a Court Leet and Court Baron held on 26 April 1682. Such courts were the origins of our democratic local government and first promoted the principle of voluntary public service. Professor G.M. Trevelyan, in his history of England, notes that they promoted stability, certainty and law, defined the services owed and the limits of the powers of the lord of the manor, exercised through his bailiff or steward. The Court Leet was in theory a royal court with the lord of the manor as the delegate of the king, and he or his steward presided over the proceedings. Through the Court Baron, the manor administered the tenancies held by favour of the lord. The tenancies were largely customary, that is originally under customs or duties of various kinds, but they were later granted by the custom of the manor and copyhold.

A number of medieval customs survived until the later years of the Court, including that of heriot, which had been a feudal service, originally military, but afterwards was the rendering of the best live beast or chattels of a deceased tenant.

Copyhold tenure, under which all tenancies were returned to the lord of the manor on the death of a holder, extended for 99 years in Seaton or for three lives.

Some extracts, taken from the survey, are shown below:

Messuage and Dwelling House. An entry, one hall, one kitchen, one dairy house and three chambers over. One barn, one stall, curtilage garden and orchard, one close called the Crosse, ½ acre. One close called the Higher Ground, 4 acres. One close called Higher Horriford, 3½ acres. One close called Higher Bottom Close, 3 acres. One close called Lower Bottom Close, 3 acres. One close called Haynes Lease, 3 acres. One close called Maunders Close with a coppice wood, 3 acres and one close called Heckstarrs, 3 acres.

One parcel of a meadow lying undivided with Elizabeth Starrs, called Pynes Meade at Common Lane, ¾ acre.

Tenants name Edward Drake. Date of lease 28 Feb 1653.
Rent 4d. The heriot £4. or best beast.
Lease 99 years – details of the lives:

Edward Drake	*63 years*
Ann his wife	*Deceased*
Edward his son	*33 years*

Dwelling house lately built by Richard Wheeler on a close of land called Beere Lane, together with the garden adjoining the said close.
Tenants name Joyce Hooper aged 52.
Date of lease 16 April 1652. Rent 4s.0d.
Heriot best goods or 10s.0d.
Lease 99 years – details of the lives

John Hooper	*Deceased*
Joyce Hooper	*his sister age 52*
Margaret Hooper	*his sister*

Messuage decayed cottage and plot of ground in Aywell Green. Liberty is given to Richard Clarke on the back-side of his lease to suffer the dwelling-house to fall down.
Tenants name Richard Clarke. Date of lease 29 Sept 1655.
Rent 5s.0d. Heriot 6s.0d.
Lease 99 years – details of the three lives

Richard Clarke	*50 years*
Richard his son	*Age 12*
Jane, his daughter	*Age 15*

One dwelling-house, a hall, a parlour, a shopp, one chamber over and one close behind the house called Netherhayes. One close called Fleethill, 2 acres, a close called Burnards Hill, 1½ acres, one close called Dunghill.
Tenants name Elizabeth Babb, 42.
Date of lease 8 Feb 1659.
Rent 6s.0d. Heriot £4.
Lease 99 years – details of three lives.

Elizabeth Babb	*Deceased*
Elizabeth Babb, 42	*her daughter, now called Elizabeth Pyke*

NB: (The choice between best beast or money as heriot was the lord's.)

Item 64 reads, 'A large parcel of Marshland called Seaton Marsh contayninge about 300 acres, 18 now in land.' The survey also contains information about the back slope of the shingle bar.

It was some time before John Willoughby's action in 1639 that a fortification was begun, in June 1627. At that time the country had a difference with France and the erection of a fort on The Burrow acted as a defence against enemies.

A great mound of earth was thrown up to erect a fort on the summit. This mound stood on the then broad shingle beach, a little to the eastward of the seafront. Originally named The Barrow, it became The Burrow. It still remains at the time of writing,

although it is incorrectly named Moridunum. At the time of building The Barrow, warrants were granted for assistance in the fortification. In the first week Colyton hundred sent 30 men every day; the next week Axminster hundred sent 30 men every day; the third week Hemyock hundred sent 20 men every day; the fourth week Halberton hundred sent 20 men every day; and in the fifth week Bampton hundred sent 20 men every day.

George Pulman, in his *Book of the Axe* (4th edition, 1875) informs the reader that 'The Barrow – as the mound, upon which Stukeley's 'Watch Tower' once stood, is now called – has of late years been almost levelled.' He can remember when it was of considerable height and size and had a billiard room upon it on the site of the ancient 'pharos'. The spot was used for centuries as a battery and had mounted guns. This four-gun battery was dismantled in 1817.

Photographs show that The Barrow was the main feature on the East Walk during the late-Victorian period, with a most attractive Victorian-style shelter on the summit. The Barrow, much maligned today, lost much of its charm through modern hands, but this former historic site could still be made an interesting heritage feature.

The revival of salt making after a lapse of nearly six centuries occurred when Sir John Trevelyan reached his majority. Over 7,000 tons of salt were used in the country every year. France was the main supplier and the French wars hit the industry very hard. Trevelyan saw this as a useful opportunity for additional revenue. The first undertaking began in Seaton in 1704, but met with disaster by 1706. A petition from an Edward Drayton of Seaton told a sorry tale of woe, including the fact that the salt tax of nearly 75 per cent meant an unfortunate start to a promising industry.

Following a new lease being drawn up on 1 July 1709, records suggest that the salt industry was now flourishing. Salt makers were usually graziers as well and at Seaton the lease of the Marshes for grazing always went with the lease of the salt works.

Salt Officers were appointed locally and they were always men of some standing. They had to put up a security of at least £200 to show that they were men above bribery. Among the inscriptions upon tablets and memorial stones in St Gregory's Church is one to an Abraham Sydenham, Salt Officer for 40 years, who died 12 November 1748 aged 69, and one to Jonathan Bawden, Salt Officer, who died 1726.

On 20 August 1723 William Stukeley sat on White Cliff to sketch what is the earliest-known view of Seaton. This view was published with his description in his *Itinerarium-Curiosum* (1724). He described the mouth of the Axe as a good half mile across. He described The Barrow on the west side near Seaton, upon a little eminence, as a modern ruined square pharos built of brick. 'They remember it 16 foot high and two guns lye there.' Stukeley also made the following interesting comments about Seaton Marsh:

More inwards towards the land beyond the great bank of beach is a marsh which the sea has made. This is full of saltpans into which they take the sea water at high tide.

In his sketch he shows four salt-pans. The salt works suggest that the industry was then flourishing but by the time Sir John Trevelyan died in 1755 and George Trevelyan inherited the title, all salt making had finished.

Sir George Trevelyan died in 1768 and his son John, who inherited the property and title at the age of 33, sold the manor in May 1788 to a Thomas Charter Esq., his solicitor and steward, but in 1836 the validity of the proceedings was called into question and a lawsuit ensued. A decree of the court in 1835 declared that the conveyance of 1788 ought to be set aside and directed a re-conveyance to the successor of the vendor of all the lands not disposed of by the purchaser previous to the filing of the bill in Chancery. This decision was confirmed on 5 September 1844 and once again the manor of Seaton came back into the Trevelyan family.

By the beginning of the nineteenth century, John Hallett, lord of the manor of Axmouth, attempted improvements at the mouth of the Axe which allowed vessels of some 100 tons to discharge their cargoes in safety. A pier was built and for some years a small-scale trade was carried on. Two schooners with mixed cargoes plied regularly between Axmouth and London. Other vessels appeared in the estuary, bringing in coal and other items. Engravings at the time show four or five vessels lying at anchor in the estuary.

For a few years life returned to the estuary, a reflection of that time in 1346 when Seaton provided Edward III with two ships and 25 men for his expedition against Calais.

On the Tithe Map of 1839 a path is shown along the back slope of the shingle bar, a dwelling is shown on The Barrow and the occupier is named as Revd John Badcock. He lived at the Manor House and would have used this property as a superior beach hut. The mansion house, with stables and gardens, stood on the site of where White Cliff flats stand at the time of writing, and was owned and occupied by a Rhoda Harbin. The Preventive Service house stood at the top of what is, at the time of writing, Trevelyan Road, and the site of Hook and Parrot was a coal yard leased by John Head. Barges landed coal on the beach and it was carried to the yard in carts.

In June 1837 the citizens of Seaton greeted the accession of Queen Victoria with enthusiastic celebrations and looked forward to a new era that would modernise outdated institutions.

THE GOODS

Above: *Joseph Good, born in Seaton in 1795, was a prominent builder, architect and at one time a banker. Highly respected and loved for his kindness, he built Check House for Sir Walter Trevelyan and Seaforth Lodge for Lady Ashburton. The Castle and Cliff Hotel, now Washington House, were also designed by him. He lived at the Castle and his children were born there. Joseph Good is pictured here with his wife and family members in the Castle, c.1850.*

Left: *Samuel Good, Seaton's first photographer, c.1869. Samuel Good was born at Seaton on 18 May 1827, the son of Joseph and Elizabeth Good. He first set up in business as a watchmaker and jeweller in Trinity Square, Axminster. Good was very keen on photography and when he moved back to premises in Fore Street, Seaton, made this interest the second part of his business. Photography must have made a tremendous impact upon the Victorians and the early photographers were all professionals. Good, apart from recording events and scenes of local interest, also took many portraits, first using the daguerreotype process and later producing cartes-de-visite, the first cheap method enabling ordinary people to have their pictures taken.*

Chapter 5

THE MID-VICTORIANS: 1840–70

The Victorian era did not open very auspiciously. An outbreak of influenza had swept over the country in 1837 and caused much suffering and death. Along with this sickness there was commercial and agricultural depression which affected most of England, including Devon.

At that time, Seaton was a small village by the River Axe which, according to the enumerator's entries in the 1841 Census, had a population of 765. Most of the working men were either agricultural labourers or fishermen, but other occupations included Henry Abbott of Streit Shear who was a lime burner, Thomas Cole of Sidmouth Street who was a sawyer, and Herman Smith of Sidmouth Street who was a cooper. There were also four shoemakers in the village. Boots were then very important for workmen and girls needed boots too – good nailed ones for use on the rough and muddy roads. Keeping one's feet dry was a necessity and shoemakers enjoyed a good trade. It is interesting to note that 50 inhabitants were over 65 years of age, including Thomas Batstone of Sidmouth Street who was 85. Seaton's oldest inhabitant, 90-year-old William Small, also of Sidmouth Street, was still working as an agricultural labourer.

Once, Seaton and its neighbour, Beer, had belonged to the abbey of Sherborne. Henry VIII sold Seaton to a John Frye of Yarty. The Trevelyan family inherited it through the marriage of the first baronet in 1655 to Mary Willoughby whose great-grandfather had bought it from his relatives, the Fryes. It was during January 1845 that the lord of the manor, Sir Walter Calverley Trevelyan, and his wife Pauline paid a long visit to Seaton. Trevelyan was then aged 47, a well-known antiquarian and geologist. His wife Pauline was 19 years younger. She was very talented and a patroness of the Pre-Raphaelites. At this time, Seaton was little changed from the eighteenth century when Polwhele spoke of it as a 'remarkably neat village in which every house has a finished air.' To Trevelyan, the neighbourhood of Seaton had interesting geological features, not least being famous for the landslip of 1839. At that time it was also considered to be the Roman station of Moridunum and this would have appealed to Sir Walter's love of history.

He decided that it was his duty to modernise Seaton by creating a spa to attract visitors of the right sort. The local bathhouse for hot and cold sea water was already in existence, but Trevelyan had it rebuilt. First-rate sewerage and an esplanade were other priorities and he spent much time and money over the next 30 years carrying out improvements in the village.

It was in August 1860 that Lady Trevelyan wrote from Seaton to William Bell Scott to say that 'Sir Walter has determined not to leave till our school is finished. Mr Woodward is also designing some seaside houses for us.' The school was finished later that year and, on its opening, Sir Walter gave the pupils a solemn address on education, ignorance and temperance. However, the major scheme for a half mile of villas along the sea front came to nothing.

Sir Walter's other plans included the installation of gas lighting, waterworks and a branch railway. He had Calverley Lodge (now Check House) built in 1864–66, which he called his cottage by the sea. It cost £3,980. The executant architect was Charles Frederick Edwards of Axminster who would have drawn on the earlier designs of Benjamin Woodward. Sir Walter was a keen early advocate of the use of concrete in building and the proposed villas would almost certainly have been of that material. Concrete was used for the Axmouth bridge and toll-house which opened in 1877.

Lady Trevelyan died on 13 May 1866 while on holiday abroad, and Sir Walter never again lived in his Seaton house. He did, however, continue his improvements at Seaton until his own death in 1879.

The Trevelyans were Cornish in origin and had been in a position of some prestige ever since an ancestor became powerful in court during the reign of Henry VI. But what about Pauline – they called her Pauline although her real name was Paulina. She was born in 1816 during the evening of Thursday 25 January. Her father was George Hermyn, the curate at Hawkedon near Bury St Edmunds, and on her mother's side she had Huguenot blood.

She was small, just over five foot, her hair was light brown, and her eyes – her main feature – hazel. She was brilliant, witty, teasing, warm, enthusiastic and tireless – a twentieth-century character among the pruderies of mid-Victorian Britain. She was a friend and patroness to many in the Pre-Raphaelite circle and played an important part in the lives of Ruskin and Swinburne in the 1850s and '60s. When

Above: *Samuel Good, Seaton's first photographer, took this picture during the summer of 1865. Only four years before that date Queen Victoria's consort, Prince Albert, had died, and before his death, Abraham Lincoln became the President of the United States. His consequent decree abolishing slavery brought about the secession of the Southern states and the outbreak of Civil War on a vast scale early in 1861. 1865 was also a year when that strong link which had so long bound the present to the past, snapped with the death of Lord Palmerston, aged 81. He had sat in the House of Commons for 58 years. The man clearing out the ditch wearing the stove-pipe hat, was a part of that world. He would not have expected his image to survive into the twenty-first century but it did, to remind us again of how quickly things change. The photograph shows the top end of Seaton's Fore Street. The building on the left with the tower is the Sir Walter Trevelyan School. Designed by Benjamin Woodward, it was built in 1860. The school was greatly remodelled in the 1960s and has lost all but one of its original lancet windows. The tower over the entrance has been reduced in height.*

A very early photograph taken by Samuel Good in 1850 of a wreck on Seaton Beach.

Ruskin was deserted by his wife Effie, for Millais, she was one of the few who stood staunchly by him. Among those in her world were the Carlyles, Tennyson, Christina Rossetti, Holman Hunt, Millais, Augustus Hare and the legendary Jane Morris, wife of William Morris, the face that inspired Rossetti in painting and poetry.

She always maintained that she liked older men so it came as no surprise when, at the age of 19, she married Sir Walter Trevelyan, 20 years her senior. He was a strange, tall, taciturn landowner-cum-scientist-cum-geologist, with a character completely opposite to hers. It was a love match and, until her early death in 1866, it was said that no husband's life could have been more identified with his wife's than Sir Walter's was by Pauline.

Pauline's strange gabled house in Seaton was known as Calverley Lodge and later, because of the chequered stonework, became Check House. It was finished in 1865 and that year Sir Walter took her to Heals to inspect modern furniture, with the furnishing of this new lodge in mind. How I would have loved to have paid a visit to Calverley Lodge at that time – I can only imagine how Pauline, with all her discrimination and knowledge of artists, would have furnished it. Certainly the pictures would have included work by Millais and Holman Hunt, with the furniture à la William Morris, whose famous precept, 'have nothing in your house that you do not know to be useful or believe to be beautiful', was the keynote of his artistic career. Pauline's early death in 1866 was a great loss to Seaton. She was a vibrant part of that Pre-Raphaelite circle, many of whom paid a visit to the town, and had she lived longer, who can tell what might have happened?

After her death, Sir Walter spent most of his time at his estate, Wallington Hall, in Northumberland. He carried on with improvements at Seaton but Pauline's vision of a modern Gothic resort never materialised. Had she lived, who knows – Seaton with all those new, wonderful buildings, a centre for the Pre-Raphaelites – could have happened.

It was at this point that Seaton moved decisively into nineteenth-century England, bringing to an end the old essentially rural social system. For the middle classes and the rich, the Victorian era was a happy age. Even the working classes had precise codes of behaviour and knew what to do on nearly every occasion that arose in life and death.

In the mid-nineteenth century, Seaton was still primarily rural with the inhabitants providing most of their own everyday needs. They built their own homes and made their own furnishings; the baker provided bread and they grew their own fruit and vegetables. Many made their own clothes but then, as now, the ladies were interested in the latest fashions and would visit the shop of Mr Agland, lace manufacturer and general draper, whose prices would bear comparison with any of the leading London fashion houses.

Henry Loud, the butcher, traded from Fore Street and also had a slaughterhouse in the town. He called on local families daily for orders and delivered free to all parts of the neighbourhood. He was noted for his dairy-fed pork. The meat fragments left over after he carved up the joints were always sold on Saturday nights, and for many families were the only meat they ever tasted.

The first Post Office in Seaton was in Fore Street and in 1840 the Postmaster was John Akerman. His father, who originally came from Burton Bradstock, combined postal duties with boat building. His boat-yard was on the site of the present Royal Clarence Hotel. In those days, the daily letters were delivered in a square, covered basket which the postman carried on his arm.

John Akerman's neighbour and friend was one of the town's greatest characters, Richard Skinner. He was a mariner and coal merchant who had travelled the world, even sailing as far as China. Richard Skinner lived at Cleve House, No. 17 Fore Street, and his coal yard was on the site of the present-day Co-op. He had six children by his wife Sarah and, according to legend, at least five more. Towards the end of his life he gave the site of his coal yard in Fore Street to the Congregational Church, possibly to make amends for his misdemeanours. Richard, who was born in Seaton on 6 April 1779, died in his native town on 2 May 1866. His wife Sarah had died in July 1827, aged 49.

The Skinner family originated from Tiverton with connections there dating back to 1711. Richard's father was also a Richard. He was born in Colyton on 25 July 1744 and died in 1819. It was during April 1847 that Richard junior bought Lions Close and Cross House Field in Fore Street. His son was later to build Salcombe House, No. 25, and Althelney House, No. 27, on the site which is next to the Town Hall at the time of writing. There were evidently old buildings near the street, probably a row of thatched cottages, which were knocked down to make way for the new houses. Mention is certainly made of larger buildings behind Salcombe House, one with a large leaded-light window. This could have been Cross House, which is mentioned in old documents but nobody seems to know where it was.

Further down Fore Street, before the Royal Clarence was built, there were old-fashioned thatched houses projecting over the road, running from The Square to Harbour Road. It was during redevelopment in The Square that John Head built two houses for his sons (the HSBC Bank and the adjoining estate agents at the time of writing). This John Head became the owner of much property in Seaton, including the coal yard which was on the site of the present-day Hook and Parrot.

The Head family had lived in Seaton since 1607, when Philip Head married the granddaughter of

Above: *Seaton Beach with the newly built Check House in the background, c.1868.*

Right: *Seaton Front, 1855. This photograph is the oldest known of Seaton and was taken by Samuel Good, the town's first photographer. On the right of the foreground is an open space (now occupied by Esplanade properties) which was Mr Head's coal yard and it was here that the coal barges left their cargo. Castle and Cliff Houses were built by Samuel's father, Joseph Good, and he gave the land to the local authorities to enable them to build Castle Hill. The uninterrupted view of fields shows Cedric House as a sentinel in the background. Note the original bathhouse in the middle foreground.*

DOWN BY THE SEA

Axmouth Harbour, c.1866.

End of West Walk, August 1870, showing West Cliff Terrace in the background. The two pillars in the foreground mark a rear entrance to Check House, or Calverley Lodge as it was then called.

FORE STREET

Looking down Fore Street, 1865.

Right: *Looking up Fore Street, c.1869. The thatched buildings on the right were then occupied by T. Sloman's posting and livery stables. Sloman's also ran the town omnibus. These stables were demolished in 1902 to make way for the new Town Hall. The shop on the corner of Cross Street was then Gould's Cross Street Machine Bakery. Gould and Son were high-class bakers and confectioners and their up-to-date bakery was fitted with all the latest machinery for the manufacture of bread.*

Left: *Fore Street, Seaton, c.1869. At the time of this photograph the house on the left in the foreground, named Prospect House, was used as wine vaults by Mitchell, Turner & Co. It was also occupied by a Mrs Hayworth, a lodging housekeeper whose husband kept a drapers shop in Fore Street. Further up the street on the left, Mr S. Gage had a family grocers shop and sold foreign and British wines. Other Fore Street traders at that time included James Skinner, a baker and confectioner, Mr Perry, furnishing ironmonger, and Edward Overmass, a joiner and builder.*

John Stockham of Branscombe, of good local stock, and went to live at Eyewell Farm. About 150 years later, John Head, who died in 1768, was a blacksmith in Seaton and it was he who commenced building the family wealth by leasing various lands and in being appointed reeve and tythingman for the manor of Seaton.

His eldest son, John Head the younger, became a merchant and, of the other sons, Robert Head became an officer in the Customs Service at the Port of Exeter. His table tomb is in Seaton churchyard. He married into the local Dare family and one of his sons, John Dare Head, also became a Customs Officer. Philip Head, another son, was one of several of the family who went to sea, and the daughter, Anne, married James Bartlett of Beer. The Barletts were another old local family who owned land in the area, including Manstones Tenement, the largest farm in Seaton.

John Head the younger was the one who started building the real fortunes of the family and he is described as a yeoman. Through his many intrigues, he became the owner of Manstones Tenement, with its lands on the west side of Seaton, and he arranged for his son, William Head, to marry Henrietta, a first cousin and daughter of his brother Philip Head, thus consolidating the family fortunes. By this time they had obtained the large coal yard in Seaton through marriage with the Culverwells, Wislades Farm from Captain Yule RN, due to a failed mortgage, Foxenholes, and the Seaton Brickyards. They developed their extensive trading interests with coal, timber, culm, etc., and as shipowners working out of Axmouth Harbour. John Head's sister Sarah married John Snook of Colyton, from whom was descended the late Bishop Mortimer of Exeter.

John Head built the two houses in The Square for his two sons. His elder son, William, married well, although he had no children. He had Wessiters House built as a gentleman's residence in 1843 and the surrounding land was laid out as parkland with a long tree-lined drive leading to the house. The second brother, John, married the daughter of William Brown, owner of the Pole Arms Inn, and he followed on at Wessiters after William's death in 1865. The third son, Robert Thomas Head, became a solicitor in Exeter and was Mayor for three years from 1864 to 1867; and his son, another Robert, married the daughter of Sir Walter Calverley Trevelyan, 6th Bart, who built Check House in Seaton. John Head of Wessiters was described in Burke's *Landed Gentry* as a gentleman and he had two sons, John Henry Horsford Head who never married, and William Brown Head who later inherited Wessiters. There was also a daughter, Henrietta, who married John Kingsbury Hole, a surgeon, and they lived at Manstones, then called Ridgeway House, followed by their son, Revd William Head Hole and his sister Marion Hole who died in 1927, when the property was sold to the Overmass family.

William Brown Head married and had one son quite late in life, who was the well-known and popular William Henry Head, who was born in 1874 and died in 1958. He was much involved in the local community and became Seaton's youngest councillor. He succeeded to all the Head properties and had a son and a daughter. The son, John Douglas Head, remained a bachelor and spent most of his life farming at Wessiters and in the locality. His sister Muriel married a Gifford but had no children. The Wessiters estate was sold up in 1959.

The Head coat of arms is described thus – sable, a chevron between three unicorns head erased, argent.

The Head family were a success story of nineteenth-century Seaton who, through hard work, many intrigues and arranged marriages, had ascended from 'trade' to 'county'.

During this period of mid-Victorian Seaton, Queen Street traders included: William Tolman, tailor and habit maker, who also 'carefully' laid carpets; Mrs J. Major, tea dealer and family grocer; R. Diment, iron and brass founder, who was also a manufacturer of cooking apparatus; and John Newbery, who had the first printing office in the area. He had considerable experience in the printing business and the first edition of W.H. Hamilton Rogers' *Wanderings in Devon* was printed by him in 1869.

Newbery was also a bookseller and newsagent. He sold *The Times* and other daily newspapers which were now arriving at the new Seaton Station on the 1p.m. train. Before the railway, newspapers were a rarity and the cost of 5d. each would have placed them beyond the reach of most people. The *Telegraph* coach which left London at five o'clock in the morning, arriving at Exeter at ten o'clock in the evening, would have left newspapers at all the principal inns on its route. As Seaton was not on the main route, by the time a copy arrived in Seaton it would have been two or three days late. The arrival of the railway would have verified the saying that 'news flies'.

Other people would leave their name in the town. Major Terrace and Violet Terrace were named after local builders. However, the village craftsmen and labourers were very much the largest class in Seaton when the enumerator, who incidentally was John Head, recorded the names on the Census of 6 June 1841. It is good to know that many of the descendants of the families listed then still live here: Abbots, Annings (who then, as now, were skilled masons), Dares, Drivers, Newtons (who were always fishermen), Millers, Searles and Turners. They all made their mark and would have known every step and turn up through Fore Street.

The opening in March 1868 of the branch line of the London and South West Railway from the junction to Seaton marked a big step forward in the history of the town and the opening ceremony was observed as a holiday. As usual, the poor were feasted.

St Gregory's

St Gregory's Church from the south-west, c.1900.

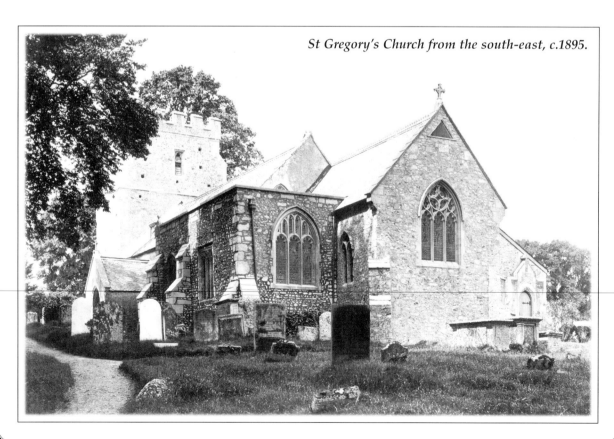

St Gregory's Church from the south-east, c.1895.

The inhabitants dined together then all marched in procession to the railway station. Flags were waved and a good time was had by all. As today, advancement leaves casualties and within a short time of the single-line railway reaching Seaton, the busy Axmouth Harbour closed to commercial shipping.

Trevelyan had left his mark on the town and, with the coming of the railway, development followed.

The town was now lit by gas, hotels had been built, new shops were opening and lodging-houses were springing up to cater for the new visitors. Seaton was now moving from a village to a resort and the golden age of tourism was about to begin. It is interesting to note that, at this stage in the town's history, there were 50 lodging-house keepers and six hotels and pubs in the town. These are listed as follows:

Lodging-House Keepers in 1870

Akerman Mrs, Post Office, Fore Street
Akerman Mrs W., 1 Bridgwater Place
Alford Mrs, Yew Terrace, Sidmouth Street
Anning Mrs John, Queen Street
Arbery Mrs, Fore Street
Bailey Mrs, 6 The Terrace
Bartlett Miss, 3 The Terrace
Batstone Mrs, The Castle
Beer Mrs, Fore Street
Brown Mrs, Sidmouth Street
Chown Mrs, Queen Street
Coles Miss A., Fore Street
Dare Mrs Bat., Fore Street
Dare Mrs E., Queen Street
Diment Mrs, Queen Street
Drew Mrs, 1 Yew Terrace, Sidmouth Street
Farrant Mrs, 2 Violet Terrace
Farrant Mrs, 3 Violet Terrace
Good Mrs, Queen Street
Hall Mrs, Bridgwater Place
Hammett Mrs, Sidmouth Street
Harris Mrs, 3 Yew Terrace, Sidmouth Street
Hayward Mrs, Windsor House and Prospect House, Fore Street
Hill Mrs, Queen Street
Hill Mrs, Fore Street
Loud Mrs F., Fore Street
Major Mrs, Queen Street
Major Miss, Fore Street

Millar Mrs G., Fore Street
Miller Mrs H., 1 Violet Terrace
Manley Mrs, Queen Street
Newbery Mrs, 1 Beach Cottage
Otton Miss E., Marine Cottage
Prescott Mrs, Woodbine Place, Sidmouth Street
Raddon Miss, Woodbine Place, Sidmouth Street
Raddon Mrs R., The Square
Rowland Mrs, Laurel Place, Fore Street
Searley Mrs, 8 The Terrace
Skinner Mrs J., Salcombe House, Fore Street
Skinner Mrs S., Melrose House, Fore Street
Stradling Mrs, 1 and 2 The Cliff
Tidbury Mrs, Queen Street
Tolman Snr Mrs, Queen Street
Tolman Mrs W., Sidmouth Street
Tucker Mrs, Fore Street
Westlake Mrs, 2 Beach Cottage
White Mrs S., Fore Street
White Mrs H., The Square
Withall Mrs, 2 Woodbine Place, Sidmouth Street
Woodgate Mrs, The Baths

Hotels, etc., in 1870

Batstone Clement, Pole Arms Hotel
Dare Bat., London Hotel
Loud William, Royal Clarence Hotel
Major William, George Inn
Oldridge John, Lion Hotel
Oldridge Timothy, King's Arms Inn

Left: *Bat. Dare, c.1865, the landlord of the London Hotel.*

Right: *Looking up Fore Street in 1862. Note the thatched cottages on the right, soon to be replaced by the Royal Clarence Hotel.*

A 'welcome home' for the Seaton Boer War heroes, 1902.

Chapter 6

THE GOLDEN AGE: 1870–1914

In considering the extensive development which followed the arrival of the railway in 1868, it is worth remembering that the shape of medieval Seaton had altered little until the changes which followed its popularity as a seaside resort. Before 1871 most Victorians went to the beach only for their health but the Bank Holiday Act of 1871 led to many social changes and gave seaside towns a new lease of life. Seaton enjoyed an increasing influx of summer visitors and when they arrived at the resort, they found a variety of apartments and newly built hotels to accommodate their needs.

In the late-nineteenth century, Seaton was still rural with the inhabitants living in what then must have been an especially beautiful village. The setting in a magnificent landscape would have attracted middle-class Victorian families seeking a quiet holiday. Yet when we look at the photographs which were taken at this time, we see how quickly and immensely things have changed.

At the turn of the century, the land known as Stony Barrow, which stretched from Trevelyan Road to Beach Road, was completely vacant and on the marsh side of Harbour Road (then Station Road), the only buildings were the railway station, Fonthill Villas, Beach Villas and the Royal Clarence Hotel. Fonthill Villas, Nos 1, 2 and 3, were then occupied by a local farmer called John Thomas, Hy Strawbridge, the stone-works manager whose wife Mary kept apartments, and a character called Billy Ware who was employed as the manor carpenter. Mr Rowdon, a tailor, lived at No. 1 Beach Villas and No. 2 was run as an apartment house by the Dyke family.

It was quite common in those days for the whole family to go on seaside holidays and stay for a few weeks, taking their servants with them. For these long holidays, middle-class England preferred to take apartments where they were allowed to eat their food in their own rooms. Here, and at resorts all around the coast, landladies were ready to cater for these visitors, thus giving the towns a new lease of life.

At the top of Harbour Road stood the Royal Clarence Hotel. Built in 1866, it was for many years a private concern run by the well-known Adams family, but in 1895 the business had merged with that magnificent sea-front hotel, the Beach Hotel.

The company directors were Mr A. Oakley of The Grove, Mr Yapp, a solicitor, and Mrs Toms of Mitchell & Thomas, the Chard brewery. Miss Plimsole was the manageress of the Clarence and a Mr Edgar was the manager of the Beach. Strange as it now seems, the magnificence of these new sea-front hotels was considered unsuitable for respectable people.

Opposite the Clarence stood Gould's staid Temperance Hotel and restaurant, on the site which is occupied by Woolworths and The Beeches Restaurant at the time of writing. C.C. Gould was one of the town's leading citizens, his restaurant a popular meeting-place for the people of Seaton.

The Bath House, which was demolished early in the twentieth century, stood in the centre of the esplanade, providing hot and cold sea-water baths. It was then run by Mrs Woodgate who charged 2s.6d. for a hot bath, 2s.0d. for a tepid bath, and 1s.0d. for a cold one. If you ordered a hot bath but did not take it, she still charged half price.

The houses in Marine Crescent were nearly all run as apartments with Mrs Henry Abbott at No. 8, Miss Effie Mayor at No. 6, and Mary Ann Welch at No. 5. This form of boarding-house was nearly always run by the lady of the house. The land from Marine Crescent to Seahill was then vegetable gardens, owned by the Woodgate family who ran the Bath House.

The Jubilee Clock, standing at the top of Seahill, was built in 1887 to commemorate Queen Victoria's Golden Jubilee. The foundation-stone was laid by the highly respected Dr Evans. A hole was cut inside the stone and in it was placed a bottle containing a set of Jubilee coins.

Castle Hill must always remain a memorial to Joseph Good, born in Seaton in 1795. He owned much of the land around Cliff House and gave a strip of it to the town for a roadway to link the Seaton sea front and Beer. Towards the end of the Victorian age, many of the houses he had built in Castle Hill were occupied by some of Seaton's leading citizens. Seafield House, destroyed by enemy action in the Second World War, stood on the site which is the Jubilee Gardens at the time of writing, and was occupied by Dr Henry Albert Pattinson. Army Captain Waring Biddle and his daughter Esme lived at

Queen Victoria's Diamond Jubilee celebrations, 1897.

Seaton Coronation Committee, King George V, 1911.

TOWN VIEWS

Above: *View of Seaton, c.1890. Note the blocks of Beer stone on the right in the foreground awaiting transport at the railway station.*

Left: *The Old Watch House which once stood at the sea end of Trevelyan Road, c.1890.*

Below: *Violet Terrace, 1895. This delightful row of houses backed on to Cross Street. They were demolished in the early 1970s to make way for the present Windsor Gardens.*

Major Terrace, 1894.

The Royal Clarence Hotel, 1896. Built in 1866, the Royal Clarence was for many years a private concern run by the well-known Adams family but by the time this photograph was taken, the business had merged with the Beach House into a limited company.

Seafield Terrace, c.1897. The field on the right, known as Sea Field, was once the site for many of the local sports meetings and celebrations.

Sidmouth Street, c.1900.

Below: *Looking down Queen Street, 1904. The shop on the right was John Real's, greengrocer and game dealer. The small cottage on the right was pulled down during 1963 and the house with the iron railings was demolished in 1982. The shop on the left right down the street was F. Tolman & Son. A jewellers and silversmiths, it remained in the Tolman family until recent years.*

Right: *Montpellier House, c.1903. Built in 1824 as a private residence, this was one of the first houses in Seaton to be built of brick so it was then known as Brick House. At the time of this picture it was occupied by Montpellier School for Girls and the name was changed to Montpellier House.*

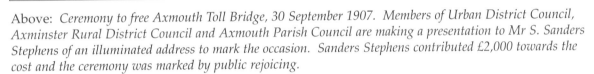

Above: *Ceremony to free Axmouth Toll Bridge, 30 September 1907. Members of Urban District Council, Axminster Rural District Council and Axmouth Parish Council are making a presentation to Mr S. Sanders Stephens of an illuminated address to mark the occasion. Sanders Stephens contributed £2,000 towards the cost and the ceremony was marked by public rejoicing.*

Opening ceremony, Seaton Town Hall, 27 July 1904.

Right: *Albert Samuel Anning, c.1909. Mr Anning was born in Seaton on 3 January 1887 and was a mason for all his working life. He was a lieutenant in the old Seaton Fire Brigade and is seen here wearing the uniform of the Seaton Territorials in which he served.*

Below: *Thornfield House, Scalwell Lane, 1908. This house was built for the private residence of E.C. Meade Esq.*

Bottom: *Looking up Harepath Road, c.1910. The town finished at the junction of Seaton Down Road with Harepath Road and the Manor Cottages on the right, built in 1901, were the last houses in Seaton. You can see the council yard in the background, standing where All Days now operate.*

Kingsland whilst Burgenstock was run as apartments by the Stradling family.

Joseph Good built Cliff Castle for himself in about 1825. He later sold it and castellated the house for the new owner. His son Zeno occupied Cliff House (now Washington House). He was born in 1838 and his half-brother Samuel was Seaton's first photographer. Zeno ran apartments at Cliff House and after his death in 1908 the business was carried on by his son, the popular Herbert Arthur Good. Members of the Mayo family were in the Castle, with a Miss James living in St Elmo.

Opposite Seafield Terrace the present-day bowling green and tennis courts (then known as Seafield) were used for grazing farm animals and Seafield was also the venue for sports-day events. Many of the houses in Seafield Terrace were also apartment houses, with Emma Loud at No. 1, Mary Rowland at No. 4, Emma Pearce at No. 11, and George Crichard at No. 14. Most of the new buildings erected in the town during the latter half of the nineteenth century were intended for the comfort, convenience and entertainment of residents and visitors, with lodging-houses and apartments providing a useful supplementary source of income.

There were no houses from Cedric Villa on the right side of Beer Road and no buildings in Darky Lane (now Marlpit Lane), except for Wessiter Lodge and Ryalls Court. In those days, when you passed Wessiter Lodge you had left Seaton and arrived in the country. This must have been a time when the English countryside was just at the peak of its beauty. The fields that generations of Seaton boys explored are now housing estates.

Part of the centre of Seaton which underwent a complete change at that time was between what is at the time of writing the Town Hall and the Pole Arms. Mr R. Fewings then owned the Pole Arms which was a family and commercial hotel. He was also the manufacturer of mineral-aerated waters. The Pole Arms had a large vegetable garden, the length of what is Marsh Road in 2002, with access through the hotel stables. These backed on to Fore Street where the launderette and adjoining shop stand at the time of writing. The site of the Town Hall was then occupied by the ginger-beer factory where Mr Fewings manufactured his mineral-aerated water and ginger beer. It was here that Harry Clapp, as a young boy, was paid 6d. a day during his school holidays to walk behind the horse which kept the machinery going. It was from stables at the Pole Arms that the Clapp family operated their posting and livery stables.

At the turn of the century there were four bus and coach operators in Seaton using horses, but by 1908 Thomas Clapp had bought up these concerns and obtained the sole privilege rights for the then London & South West Railway. Thomas Clapp was born in 1852 and died in 1938, and he was one of the town's great characters. His personal runabout was a pair of trotting ponies attached to a brilliant yellow drosky. His normal attire comprised highly polished brown boots and leggings, black and white check breeches, a red waistcoat, a brown Norfolk jacket, and with these he sported white mutton-chop whiskers.

On the opposite side of the road, in Bank House, lived a man with the splendid name of Alfred D'Angibau. He was the manager of the Wilts. and Dorset Bank in The Square. Next to Bank House, on the corner of Fore Street and Cross Street, was William Gould & Son, established as far back as 1832. Gould claimed that his was the best bread, manufactured under the highest hygienic conditions in one of the most up-to-date bakeries in Devon. They still made wonderful bread and cakes right up to the 1970s.

Shopkeepers at that time were individualists and were there to serve and give their best. Fore Street was then the home of many cheerful faces and characters, with people like James Perry, ironmonger, tinman and brazier, who was also a dealer in looking-glasses and toys and had his household store where the opticians is at the time of writing. His son, who went by the name of 'Tinker' Perry, was the well-known artist Arthur Perry whose watercolours of Seaton and Beer are much sought-after today. There was John Hayward, the shoemaker, and the Folletts who were truly old-fashioned grocers. They would have worn the traditional long white aprons, and no doubt when you passed their shop you would have noticed the delicious aroma of coffee mixed with the smell of smoked bacon and spices. When people called at these shops, nothing was too much trouble – credit was given to customers and great deference was shown by the shopkeeper to the carriage trade.

Fore Street was also the home of one of the town's best-loved figures, for it was at Netherhayes that Dr George Evans lived. The 'good old doctor', as he was generally called by Seaton people, was a wise counsellor and a staunch friend to all. He performed many generous acts and, when he died on 9 December 1902 at the age of 76, the town closed in mourning. In those days, all the men of the town would line up outside the house where there had been a death – an old custom called the walking funeral. At the 'good old doctor's' funeral, over 150 men walked behind the coffin in twos, all in top hats and black clothes. It must have been a moving sight.

Further down Fore Street, in The Square, was Good the watchmaker. He lived in the house that is the HSBC Bank at the time of writing. Also in The Square was the shop of Seaton chemist Charles Frederick Gosney, although his correct address was 11 Marine Parade. He provided surgical appliances, homeopathic medicines, patent medicines and the famous Gosney's 'Neuralgic Mixture', which he sold in vast quantities at 1s.6d. a bottle.

Seaton Villa, now Eyre House in Queen Street, was the residence of a Dr Eyre. Queen Street at the close of the nineteenth century remained much as it

CONGREGATIONAL CHURCH

Laying the foundation-stone of the new
Congregational Church in Cross Street,
21 September 1894.

Laying the foundation-stone of the Congregational Church in Cross Street, 1894.

Members of the Seaton Congregational Church in Cross Street gather outside the church for this group photograph, dated about 1907. The occasion is unknown.

DOWN TO BUSINESS

Right: *The Clapp family were in transport in Seaton for over 100 years. The three generations of the family who ran the firm are pictured here. Thomas, the founder of the firm, is sitting on the chair with his son, Harry, standing behind him. Harry's grandson, Geoffrey, is sitting on Thomas' knee. Geoff Clapp, who died in 1990 aged 79, was the last member of the family in the business.*

Below: *Clapps Transport, Seaton, c.1912. The pair of horses and wagonette driven by Harry Clapp were pictured leaving Manor Road for the Lambert Castle races.*

James William Skinner and his wife Sarah with daughter Ada pictured at the rear of Salcombe House, Fore Street, 1899. James, who died in 1913 aged 87, lived at Salcombe House and ran a bakery business from there. He was also the owner of the Golden Lion Inn in Fore Street. Daughter Ada never married and died in 1945 aged 87.

Mr D.F. Gosney and family members, c.1901. Gosney ran the town's chemist shop in Marine Place, Seaton until his death in 1935. He was famous for his home-made medicines, such as Gosney's Neuralgic Mixture, Gosney's Bronchial Syrup and Gosney's Corn Cure which reputedly cured corns within a few applications. One gets the impression from his early advertisements that, if one had it, Gosney could cure it. One of his two daughters was Eileen Gosney who died in 1988 after devoting her life to researching the history of her native town. She was a founder member of the Axe Valley Heritage Museum.

Seaton Group, c.1895. Although we know the names of this group of Seaton dignitaries pictured by local photographer G.W. Barton, the occasion is unknown. Left to right back row: Harry Abbott, Harry Jones (the postman), C.J. Gosney (the chemist), J.G. Oldridge (the schoolmaster), Mr Stickland (the bank manager), Samuel Good (the photographer), R. Follett (the store-keeper), W. Badcock (the carter), front: Parson Beale, Doctor Evans, Parson Richardson.

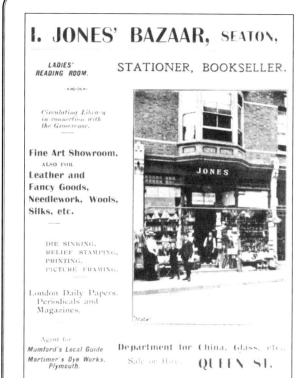

Above: *Construction of Lloyds Bank, c.1909.*

Left: *An advertisement for Jones' Bazaar, 1901.*

Seaton rugby team, 1894–95 season – the first season that they played as a team.

had looked 60 years earlier. No. 9 was then the home of the well-known Abraham Tidbury who kept apartments. His father was Isaac Tidbury, the last Trinity House pilot to work in Axmouth Harbour. Trading at No. 13 were Tolman & Son, jewellers and silversmiths. William Hayman Overmass, the undertaker and upholsterer, was also in Lower Queen Street. He also undertook removals to all parts by road or rail. They are now part of a vanished world, and I am sad to relate that the Tidburys, the Overmasses and the Tolmans, who were then members of Seaton's oldest families, no longer exist.

Although this part of England is not so renowned for bands as the Midlands and the North, Seaton at that time could boast not only a Town Band but also a Boys' Brigade Band. It was in Queen Street that Tom Perry lived, the bandmaster of the Boys' Brigade, so the residents of this part of Seaton were often treated to band selections from the boys. Unfortunately it is not known if this was appreciated by his neighbours.

The junction of Beer Road and Queen Street, on the site of the old Library, the Post Office and Axe Valley Insurance, was once the farmhouse of Lowman's Farm. The farmyard was where the old SWEB showrooms stand at the time of writing. The farm belonged to our Mr Roy Chapple's great-great-great-grandfather, Joseph Bartlett. However, by 1900 the farm on the corner was called Ridgeway House and belonged to John Kingsbury Hole. Ridgeway House was bought in 1927 by John Overmass and in 1957 Roy Chapple's father bought the Overmass business, which then traded as Overmass & Chapple. So, after a break of nearly 150 years, the property passed back to the Chapple family again.

A short step across the road and we are now in Cross Street. It was on 21 September 1894, on the site of the old Hardings Dairy, that the foundation-stone for the new Congregational Church was laid. This church, built at a cost of £2,400, replaced the smaller chapel in Fore Street, which had been built in 1825. Cross Street was also the home of another wonderful Seaton character, fisherman Timothy Gosling, who lived next to the church. His neighbours included Charlie Real and quarry foreman Harry Abbott.

The streets of Victorian Seaton had a patina of dust and mud, laced with horse droppings. The dirt must have trailed into homes on skirt hems and shoes, providing work for people like Mrs Hatchley who kept a laundry in Cross Street and whose hands and bare arms were white and shrivelled from always being in the soap suds.

Back to Sidmouth Street, which then commenced at Beer Road corner. The bottom end looked much the same, although some of the buildings have changed, notably the thatched cottages next to Ridgeway House have been replaced with the shops which stretch from Marshalls shoe shop to the Sweet Shop at the time of writing.

It was in Sidmouth Street that, in 1889, local builders White and Newbury built the Church of the Good Shepherd at a cost of £1,250. The Church of England was central to the life of the town and church-going was flourishing. The Parish Church could not always seat the great congregation and in winter was too far away for the elderly to attend evening service. Indeed, right up until the First World War, the evening service always took place at the Good Shepherd. The Victorian faith in the truth of Christianity gave them the assurance that it would overwhelm all the other religions in the world. This, of course, was not the case and although we still look to the Church for christenings, weddings and funerals, regular church-going is something different. The congregation dwindled and this sadly meant that the Church of the Good Shepherd became redundant. It was sold during the 1970s to become the offices of John Wood and the local Masonic Lodge.

Below the Church of the Good Shepherd were three tiny thatched cottages, now long gone, which at the turn of the century were occupied by fishermen Bussy Tower, Jack Hooper and Billy Power Benham. It was about this time that Jack Hooper returned home from a fishing trip to find his house on fire. All his furniture had been saved by neighbours and was out on the opposite pavement. Jack was also a keen gardener and under the staircase he had three trays of seed potatoes ready for planting. Helpers had emptied them all into one box and Jack, seeing what had happened, shouted out 'Who was it mixed all me dam teddies – shouldn't I like to catch um.' After a moment he then came out with 'Oh, is my old woman all right?'

Still in Sidmouth Street we pass Woodbine Place with its row of charming cottages – I am happy to say that this piece of old Seaton still remains to delight. These cottages were the first Coastguard homes to be built in the town. At the dawn of the new century, Major Terrace was occupied by better-class Seaton, with the Bank family in No. 1 and Mrs Burton in No. 2. In No. 3 lived two well-known ladies, the Misses Needs, who dressed in the Victorian style until they died in the 1930s. No. 4 was occupied by Col Tinley, in No. 5 lived Captain John Sackville Swann, and No. 6 was the home of the Miller family.

Much of the rest of Sidmouth Street to Manor Road has changed beyond recognition and, I am sad to say, not for the better. The exception is Stock Lane which remains another of Seaton's hidden treasures. Back at the turn of the century, Stock Lane was well known to all of the town's wrongdoers, for it was here that the formidable PC Friend lived, Seaton's only policeman. Just before Stock Lane is Montpellier, an imposing building which was once known as Brick House. It got its name because when it was built in 1824 it was one of the first houses in the town constructed with brick. It later became Friedenheim School for Girls but by the turn of the century was

Seaton Town Band, c.1900.

*Carnival tableau by Seaton Rugby Club in preparation, c.1896. The photograph was taken at
The Wessiters, the residence of W.H. Head Esq.*

Seaton cricket team, c.1900. Players include: *Tom Rodgers, Sam Rodgers, Harry Jones,
Anthony Hooper, Bert Agland, Billy Head.*

*Seaton rugby team, c.1904. Left to right, back row: Horatio Evan (licensee of the George Inn), ?,
Bill Snell, Sam Real, Fred Abbott, Nobby Snell, ?, Harry Jones (the postman), ?;
middle row: Sam Rodgers, George Rodgers, ?, Herman Cawley, Bill Real (the local gas-lamp lighter);
front row: Tom Harding, W.H. Head, ? Real.*

*Seaton cricket team, c.1905. Although the origin of the club is lost in the mists of time, it is known that the
first pavilion was erected in 1879 and cost £50. It was blown down and rebuilt in 1897 when Dr Pattison
was secretary and treasurer. The team pictured here were local men playing in a match against visitors.
Players included: W. Head, ? Loud, H. Jones, S. Rodgers, Bill Robins and W. Agland.*

Mr W.H. Head and the crew of his sailing boat, Grace Darling, c.1906. Mr Head is pictured here sitting in the middle of his boat with his crew who were members of the Seaton fishing family of Newton.

Members of Seaton Rugby Club sitting on Mr W.H. Head's racing skiff.
Mr Head is sitting in the middle holding a silver cup.

Seaton Rugby Football Club, 1912/13 – winners of the Devon Junior and Coronation cups.

SCOUT MOVEMENT

The first Boy Scout Troop was formed in Seaton during April 1913 and Scouts were sworn in on May 5th. 1913. The Scout Master was A. R. Wyatt.. Asst. Scout Masters were W. Giles and W. Newton.. Chaplin – Rev. R.S.Robinson. Secretary – A.G.J.Jackson.

LAND SCOUTS

FOX PATROL

J. Hayward   Leader
F. Salter   Second
W. J. Clegg
F. Jones
S. Hooper
C. Northcote

CUCKOO PATROL

C. Savage
G. Stickland
J. Newton
F. Scott
H. Warden
C. Mutter

OWL PATROL

G. Northcote Leader
C. Sutton   Second
P. Ball
F. Miller
B. Gigg
G. Driver

KANGAROO PATROL

A. Real
L. Stockland
G. Slade
E. Richards
W. Ball
L. Smith

SECOND CLASS SCOUTS

A. Real
G. Northcote
C. Savage
C. Watts
F. Salter
H. Sutton
G. Sutton
L. Hooper
E. Richards

F. Scott
J. Hayward
L. Stockland
G. Stickland
P. Eeles
F. Jones
F. Miller
G. Driver

SEA SCOUTS

OTTER PATROL

P. Eeles   Leader
L. Hooper   Second
A. Ostler
R. Ostler
W. Littley
W. Real

SEAL PATROL

C. Watts   Leader
F. Restorick Second
V. Osborne
J. Watts
W. Newton
B. Fewings

WOLF CUBS

(Formed March 5th. 1914)

H. Sutton   Leader
W. Wyatt   Second
L. Northcote
W. Jones
L. Martin
J. Real
J. Fillbrook
E. Littley
A. Turner
A. Newton
G. Presset

Left: *Seaton Scouts, Vicarage Field, Seaton, c.1913. In August 1907, 20 boys led by two men pitched their tents on Brownsea Island in Dorset. The boys were gathered from all walks of life and for two weeks they learnt to live in the open and to cultivate comradeship. From this small beginning the Boy Scout movement was born and Baden Powell, their leader, was on his way to becoming a world figure. The first Seaton Boy Scout troop was formed during April 1913 and there we have some of the first Scouts, with Chaplain Revd R.S. Robinson.*

RURAL LIFE

*Haymaking in the Vicarage Field, Seaton, c.1909. The present-day Case Gardens were built on the Vicarage Field and in this photograph some of the men of Seaton are working at haymaking. **Left to right:** Messrs Long, Newton, Pearce, Real, Peach, Sellars and Chant. The little boy is one of the Peach family.*

Stoke Hill Foot Beagles meet at Seaton, c.1908. The Beagles hunted hares and local supporters shown here had gathered to follow the day's sport. The stone building in the background is now R. Dack's workshop and was the only building in Court Lane at that time. Note the elm trees on the right of the photograph; it was never realised how important and characteristic a place in the Engish countryside the elm tree held until their virtual disappearance from Dutch elm disease.

THE WATERFRONT

Seaton Beach looking west, 1880.

Axmouth Harbour, c.1880.

Above: *Seaton Beach and the Bath House looking east, c.1890. The Bath House seen here in the centre provided residents and visitors alike with hot and cold sea-water baths.*

Seaton Beach, 1895. The Bath House can be seen on the right and next to it is Seafield House which was destroyed by a German bomber during the Second World War. On the left is Cliff Castle. This was built by Joseph Good in 1825.

Right: *Seaton Esplanade, 1899.*

Seaton Beach, 1895.

Seaton Hole, c.1890.

Lew Hollow, Seaton Hole, 1895.

Seaton Beach Hotel, Seaton, Devon.

E. A. & C. C. SMITH, Proprietors.

Within five minutes' walk of the Railway Station

Three-and-a-half hours from Waterloo.

Special Terms for Winter Visitors.

New Heating Arrangements.

FIRST CLASS FAMILY HOTEL. Stands on the Esplanade, and commands an uninterrupted view of the whole of the magnificent Bay between Berry Head and the Bill of Portland.

Advertisement for the Seaton Beach Hotel, 1900.

This photograph, taken before 1900, shows the red granite drinking fountain which rested on a base of grey granite and stood on the seafront. The fountain was presented to the town by Mr and Mrs W.H. Willans as a memorial to the long reign of Queen Victoria. It was formerly unveiled by Mrs Willans in the presence of about 200 inhabitants of the town on Friday afternoon, 27 August 1897.

Seaton Beach, 1903. Gwendoline Marsh was a member of a solid, established, professional family. Her father was a solicitor in Yeovil. Every year the family took their holidays in Seaton and when they came in 1903, Gwendoline took this enchanting picture of the children of family friend Elsie Howse.

Left: *Visitors on Seaton Beach sitting in front of the old West Walk shelter, 1900.*

Steamers landing at Seaton, c.1898. During the summer season, Cosen's & Co. Steamers, from Weymouth, made frequent calls at Seaton, giving the visitors the opportunity to enjoy trips to Sidmouth, Torquay, Dartmouth and up the 'English Rhine' as the coast trip was then described. Steamers also came up the Channel from Exmouth.

Landing passengers at Seaton, c.1904. The pleasure steamer, Victoria, conveyed passengers to Bournemouth and Weymouth from Torquay, calling on its way at Sidmouth, Seaton and Lyme Regis. Although these towns had no pier, passengers got ashore via a small bridge thrown out to the beach from the boat.

known as Montpellier School.

At the top of Manor Road, on the site of the Seaton Evangelical Church in 2002, was the workshop of Jim Pearce, the wheelwright. With the disappearance of farm wagons, the wheelwright's craft was sadly lost. They had the instinct that only survives today among the older craftsmen: the 'rule of thumb', a compound of experience, taste and sound judgement which owed nothing to theories or books. The old saying went, 'a good carpenter could never make a bad wheelwright but a bad wheelwright could make a good carpenter.' Needless to say, Jim Pearce and his staff were excellent wheelwrights.

Still in Sidmouth Street, we pass the old infants' school and Manor Cottages. The old infants' school, then occupied by the manor for use as their estate office, was also where the old Local Board met. At that time the part-time clerk was solicitor Mr A.P. Cann Evans, assisted by Mr Ernest Skinner who acted in nearly every other capacity. In those days this was where Seaton ended – no Highwell Road, no Townsend, no Eyewell Green, no Mooracre, no houses in Scalwell Lane, and nothing except Shepherds Cottage and Louds slaughterhouse in Harepath Road.

Back down Court Lane, which was then devoid of any buildings, we arrive at the cricket field. The first games were played here during May 1875, against Colyton and Exeter. The first captain and hon. sec. of the club was Dr H. Pattinson and in 1884, as a testimonial for his valuable services, a subscription list was opened and met with a ready response from 82 members and friends. He was presented with a gold watch and chain and his wife was presented with a gold chain.

At the bottom of Court Lane, the building which was converted into flats during the late 1990s by Ross Dack was a slaughterhouse, and Case Gardens opposite was then the Vicarage Field. At the turn of the century, the vicar of Seaton was the saintly Revd Richardson. If the church was there to cater for spiritual needs then the nearby Kings Arms catered for bodily ones. It was here on Saturday nights that landlady Sarah Salter served locals in the smoky taproom, listening to Ned Parsons with his accordion bringing many a forgotten country song back to life over glasses of beer.

Tudor House, opposite the Kings Arms, was then occupied by another local fisherman, Mr T. Hooper, and in those days, between Tudor House and the school were stables belonging to the Beer Free Stone Quarries. Opposite the school, where Fortfield Terrace stands at the time of writing, were allotments called Barn Hay. Locals could rent a plot for 1s.6d. a year which was paid on Lady Day at the Manor Estate Office, now the Women's Institute. Moving down to Fore Street to the corner of Manor Road, there was a blacksmith's workshop belonging to William Henry Oldridge. He was an expert blacksmith as well as a farrier – he would have learned his craft from his father. The job would have come as second nature to him, the knowledge in the blood as much as in the brain.

It was in the 1890s, fresh from Caius College, Cambridge, that young Bill Head formed the Seaton Rugby Club. Players in this highly successful club included Bill Real, Tom Harding, Dan Searle, Dr Monty May, Dicky Skinner, Tom Rodgers, Jack Jones, Fred Trinnemen, Herman Cawley, Jess Hooper, Fred Pearce and the legendary local fisherman, Nobby Snell. Nobby was capped for the county and became a first reserve for the England team. It remains a mystery to me why rugby was replaced by football in Seaton after the First World War.

The Victorian era ended on the evening of 22 January 1901 when the people of Seaton heard that Queen Victoria, surrounded by her children and grandchildren, had died. It was the beginning of a new century and Seaton was enjoying a prosperity they would never again achieve. With seven hotels and numerous lodging-houses, the resort had many simple delights to please old and young alike. During the summer months, visitors could take sea trips on Cosen's & Co. Steamers from Weymouth, visiting places such as Sidmouth, Torquay, Dartmouth and Weymouth, and enjoying the special views of the Dorset and Devon coastline.

In those halcyon days of the late-Victorian and early-Edwardian age, the local *Pulmans Weekly News* published lists which recorded the names of visitors who were staying at the various hotels and boarding-houses. Surviving copies of this publication provide a unique record of those leisurely days. The seaside holiday had become an annual event for all who could afford it, although resorts like Seaton depended chiefly on the middle classes and retired, for the upper classes went abroad or spent long weekends with each other in the country.

Seatonians (people who were born in the town) took a great pride in Seaton. Even with the great range of the dissimilarity of its inhabitants – the wealthy, the middle class, the doctor, the plumber, the fisherman, the farm labourer and the hotelier – they all had a bond, a community spirit, a respect for each other's abilities or shortcomings. In those days, because the majority of people were not only born in Seaton but worked and raised children in the town, the community was much more rounded and complete. This was a time when people provided their own entertainment; there was no radio or television, very few cars on the road, no frenzied race against time.

During the Edwardian period, two milestones in the town's history occurred. Great excitement was felt by all when the first motor car arrived in the town. It belonged to Fred Diment and when he really drove the car to its limits, it reached speeds of 20 miles per hour. The vehicle had tiller steering.

SIR WALTER TREVELYAN SCHOOL

Pupils of Sir Walter Trevelyan School, c.1895. The headmaster, Mr Oldridge, is standing on the left.

*Sir Walter Trevelyan School class, 1902. The teachers then were headmaster, Mr Oldridge,
who was assisted by Miss Paye and Miss Gush.*

Sir Walter Trevelyan School football team, c.1908.

The staff of Sir Water Trevelyan School, c.1922. Left to right: Miss Elizabeth Gosling, Mrs Oldridge (headmaster's wife), Jenks White, Mr Oldridge (headmaster), Miss Tozer.

Diment was to open the first garage in Station Road, now Harbour Road, in 1905. The other notable event was the opening of Seaton Town Hall on 27 July 1904. The Town Hall, built by Seaton builders G.H. Richards, soon became the social centre of the town and our motorist friend, Mr Diment, was the first manager of the Town Hall Company.

The Edwardian period ended when King George V came to the throne in 1911. The coronation was an occasion of national rejoicing and a full pro-gramme of celebrations was arranged in Seaton. The streets were lavishly decorated and at midday there was a grand proces-sion followed by sports. Mr C.C. Gould provided a grand buffet lunch in a marquee on The Burrow for all the inhabitants – the mouth-watering menu included roast beef, roast lamb, boiled beef, veal pie, pressed beef, English ham, ox tongue, hot potatoes, salads and pickles. This was followed by gooseberry tart, plum pudding, mixed fruit, plum tart and Devonshire cream, and you could

This picture looking west in 1875 gives a clear view of Westcliff Terrace long before the Chine was built.

wash all that down with ale, cider, lemonade and ginger ale. Clifford Gould was a man who lived for Seaton and its people – this lunch was typical of a man who lived by service and not self.

Leisure facilities for locals were greatly improved and Seaton continued as a thriving town. However, 1914 was the end of those golden summers. The threat of war that had been hanging over Europe reached a climax on 4 August when Sir Edward Grey, the Minister of Foreign Affairs, stood up in the House of Commons and declared war against Germany. For the first time since Napoleon, war became more than an adventure in foreign parts.

Much excitement was felt by the people of Seaton, since local men were serving in the Army, the Navy and also the Reserves. War fever swept the town but few realised that this war would last four long years, or that the devastation and slaughter would be worse than anyone could imagine.

Seaton East Walk and the Beach Hotel, 1895.

Peace celebrations on The Burrow, 1919.

Chapter 7

THE FIRST WORLD WAR: 1914–18

During the first days of the First World War there was a steady enrolment of men from Seaton. The first Sunday after the declaration of war, 9 August 1914, was set apart as a day of intercession for divine mercy and the safety of the Empire. The Parish Church of St Gregory's was crowded and the impressive service, conducted by Revd Robinson, closed with the singing of the National Anthem.

The day before war was declared was the August Bank Holiday Monday and on that day – a day of unclouded sunshine – hundreds of people gathered in The Square and along Station Road to see the Army and Navy reservists leave by special trains. Thanks to a well-prepared operation called the War Book, everyone knew what to do. All reservists would have received that day a telegram with only one word – 'mobilise' – and with this they could obtain a rail warrant to their destination.

In the early days of the war, the uneventful life of the town was shaken by two things. The first was a dreadful explosion in Violet Terrace, caused by a gas leak. No one was injured but much damage was done. The second event, on Tuesday 11 August, was even more exciting for the townsfolk. Two German spies had been arrested and taken to the Town Hall Police Station where a large crowd gathered to see them taken to Exeter by motor car. Nothing is known of their fate.

To assist with the war effort, the National War Savings Committee was appointed by the Treasury to encourage thrift. Many other organisations helped in this effort and in Seaton Mr F.R. Plowman, the local secretary of the National Deposit Friendly Society, opened a War Fund and appealed to his members for monthly penny contributions. Records show that the people of Manor Cottages were most supportive, with a Mr W. White at No. 10 paying 1s.0d. a month, Mr Hine at No. 4, Mrs G. Real at No. 5, and Mr and Mrs G. Peach at No 1. paying 3d. a month. It is good to note that members of the Peach family still live at No. 1 – they must hold the record for the longest occupation of a house in Seaton by the same family.

For the duration of the war James Skinner's daughter, Ada, kept a diary and noted interesting events that took place in the town. She recorded that Friday 6 November 1914 was a glorious day, quite hot. Seaton was in a state of great excitement with flags flying everywhere. A total of 250 Army recruits had marched from a camp at Honiton on an exercise and the Seaton Town Band, with the Scouts, met them and they all marched to the seafront and then up Fore Street to the Town Hall for refreshments. One can imagine that, after the refreshments and the marching around Seaton to the cheers of locals, it would seem a long way back to Honiton.

Miss Skinner also recorded the loss of HMS *Formidable*, a pre-war dreadnought battleship that carried a complement of 790 officers and men. On 1 January 1915 she was struck by a torpedo at about 1.30a.m., some miles off the Devon coast. She sank an hour and a half later. Owing to the rough sea and intense cold, there were only about 200 survivors.

During those terrible days of 1915 and 1916 casualty lists were heavy. It was during the great offensive of the Somme, when 19,000 British soldiers were killed on the first day of the battle, that Seaton fishermen who were out at night said that they saw angels over White Cliff.

The war years were a time of great hardship and sadness, and local people – with their minds full of danger – saw suspicious meanings in everything. Rumours swept the town and this placed a heavy burden on the local police as, besides having to deal with all the many new regulations, they had to investigate all reports, no matter how ridiculous.

Much war work was undertaken by volunteers and a local unit of the Voluntary Aid Detachment (VAD) was formed in Seaton before the war. Many of these volunteers were to serve at Ryalls Court which became a military hospital. Most of the patients were fairly straightforward but there were some with multiple gunshot wounds. Dr Edward Tonge from Beer was the principal medical officer in charge of the hospital and, for his work during the war years, he was awarded the OBE. One member of the Seaton VAD was Muriel Head, the only daughter of William from the Wessiters. Like many daughters of well-to-do families, Muriel became a VAD nurse during the First World War. She was posted to No. 7 Military Hospital at Streatham Hall. Although the VAD nurses worked entirely voluntarily, they were much involved in the hard reality of wartime nursing and by the end of the war had proved their usefulness. They were loved by convalescing soldiers who teasingly interpreted the VAD as 'Very Artful Darlings' or even 'Victim Always Dies'. Some of Muriel's patients corresponded with her after they left hospital and many fell in love with her. By the 1920s most of the letters had ceased but those from a young officer, whom we know only as Teddy, continued until 1926. The indications are that she fell in love with Teddy and that they became engaged, although it seems that in the late 1920s he died so the marriage never went ahead. One letter reveals that he had a throat problem and had been told to give up smoking.

Family documents show that Muriel remained single until the Second World War when she married Col Ralph Gifford who was running a factory engaged on war work at Chard and who, I understand, had been an officer in the First World War. Muriel went to London to train in canteen management and later ran a wartime factory canteen. Affectionate letters to Muriel from her officer friend, Teddy, show that the latter moved in the same London social circles as the then Prince of Wales, who was destined briefly to become King Edward VIII. In a letter written in 1925, Teddy tells of a house party attended by the Prince in a house called Craven Lodge. He wrote:

The Craven Lodge show was a wonderful one. The Prince arrived home at 1.20a.m. having driven from London. He was tired and well lubricated so he spoke to one or two people and went to bed. The next day he hunted all day and then motored to London for another official dinner. The dance was a very cheery one indeed. As they looked upon it as rather private, they didn't seem to mind what they did. The crowd was much more exclusive even than the Hunt Ball. The Prince's own staff were in attendance, along with some waiters, an expert oyster man and a caviar merchant. The buffet was gorgeous and the special 'royal cocktail' was a very deceptive one. I have never seen more drinking. Major Barnaby auctioned a horse for over £400 and two pups, one for £40 and the other £30, in a very brilliant manner, though he may have been a bit personal with several of the celebrities. Mrs Wardell (one of the Prince's lady friends) was very much there, of course. The latest has been Mrs Dudley Coates but she has broken her leg. The royal affections have been transferred to Mrs Montague. Craven Lodge is much nicer than it looks. It is beautifully furnished and it seemed a shame to see cigarette ends all over such lovely Persian carpets. We are having dreadful weather, gales and rain, but today is gorgeous. I hope you are careful and not getting wet. We have heaps of 'flu. Give mummy [Muriel's mother] my love and I have lots and heaps for you.

Muriel's correspondence indicates that she was an accomplished ballroom dancer and her admirers liked to partner her. Teddy, in another letter, said he was looking forward to attending a dance with her in Exeter and had been taking dancing lessons. He would be staying at the Rougemont Hotel. But he revealed that a throat specialist had found problems due to smoking and that he was trying to give it up (whether that might have been the cause of his premature death is open to speculation). He also told Muriel that he had sold the sidecar from his motorcycle combination and had bought a new one with a windscreen and something to keep the mud off, and thought she would like riding it much better.

Among Muriel's earlier correspondence was an RAF officer who wrote in 1917:

Dear Mu, I am just snatching a few minutes from my multifarious duties in connection with the Great War to let you know how hard I have been working since I left Exeter, ahem! I got all the men and heavy transport down to Portsmouth on Tuesday and came down myself yesterday with the last two Crossley touring cars, a most imposing sight, beetling through villages at an average of 31mph the whole way. I know you are working hard but try and find time to write to me sometimes. I always look forward to your letters. My address in a week's time will be 85 Wing, Independent Force, RAF, BEF, France.

A Royal Artillery officer, back with his unit in 1918, wrote:

My dearest little girl. I so loved to receive your letter. I am still smiling about your 'pal' reference. You dear, loyal soul. I am quite happy to have you for a pal and if you won't give me more than that, I'll have to be content, though God knows how I want your love. So we are pals and you like me and I love you. It is sweet of you to say you missed me dreadfully and I do hope you really meant it...

Another Artillery officer, writing just after Christmas 1918, told her, 'There are so many officers away on leave that we poor unfortunates who are here have plenty to do to occupy their time.' He ended, 'Always, your devoted Alan.' In a later letter, Alan, now out of the Army, tells her he has started training as a dentist and asks her to write to him at the Royal Dental Hospital, Leicester Square, London. He said:

With no failures in any of the exams it will still take me four years to complete the course. But taking into account that I never was the possessor of more than a rather below the average amount of brains – and that those got horribly rusted during four years in the Army – I have rather serious doubts about whether four years will see me through or not.

Rather more formal was a letter in May 1919 from a man who had moved from Streatham Hall to a convalescent home for officers in Kent. He enclosed a copy of a photograph he had taken of her and added:

THE WAR YEARS

Above: *Seaton, 1914. At the outbreak of the First World War, Seaton soon began to buckle on her armour and the normally quiet seaside town became a continuous scene of bustle and excitement. The steady enrolment of men proceeded week by week and in this picture we see some of the first men who joined the Devonshire Regiment marching down Sea Hill during the late-summer of 1914. We do not know how many of them came back; we know only too well that too many of their generation died and those that did return found England had changed beyond recognition. Over 200 men from Seaton served in the conflict and of these, 24 made the supreme sacrifice. Their bodies lie in many lands, beneath many seas but their names are recorded on the memorial cross which stands by the entrance to the old Parish Church, reminding all future generations of what they gave fighting for a cause they believed would lead to a better world.*

Right: *Reginald Wilkie Gosney. The son of a Seaton chemist, Reginald Gosney became a Second Lt in the First World War. He was on the Indian Army Reserve of Officers attached to the 76 Punjabis and in 1915 was transferred to Mesopotamia where he took part in the capture of Kut and the ill-advised advance to Baghdad. After the capture of Kut, the British Forces, with a rifle strength of 13,000, advanced to attack the Turkish position at Ctesiphon. The Turks numbered more than 18,000 and after the battle on 22 November 1915, the British retreated with a loss of more than 4,500 men. Casualties and the dead were either left or buried by the Turks with no regard to identification. Lt Gosney, who was mentioned in Dispatches, was killed in the battle of 22 November and his name is inscribed on the Basra Memorial in Iraq to those who have no known grave.*

Sad to relate I have not been to a dance since I left Exeter. How did you enjoy the Peace Ball. I just missed it. Just my beastly luck. I am playing golf with one hand at present and rather erratic. But I would far rather have dancing. I was very triste at having to leave without saying goodbye to you. Still, if these people will send one off at 12 hours notice!...

Another Army officer wrote in October 1918 that he had been hoping for a posting to Palestine, but seemed more likely to be posted back to France. He signed off, 'Don't forget to write when you've a moment, will you dear, as it'll buck me up a lot.'

New Zealand and Canadian officers were also among Muriel's admirers. Many New Zealanders were patients in Exeter's war hospitals.

After being left a widow in the 1950s and disposing of her parents' home, Wessiters in Seaton, Muriel moved to a comparatively modest house in the town which was her home until she died in the early 1990s.

By the spring of 1917 food shortages became acute and it was a common thing to see long queues of people outside the butcher's shop waiting their turn to be served. There was also a great scarcity of potatoes, and white bread was a thing of the past. This became so serious that on Thursday 24 May, the King's proclamation regarding the shortage of food was read outside the Town Hall. This caused great excitement in the town and crowds of people gathered to hear the proclamation.

By 1918, it seemed as if the war would never end and news from the Front was anxiously awaited. In Seaton, as elsewhere, there was a growing shortage of coal and a new Household Fuel and Lighting Order came into operation in August 1918. Sunday 4 August 1918 was the National Remembrance Day, on the fourth anniversary of the declaration of war against Germany. A service in the Parish Church was followed by a gathering in The Square, where the hymn 'O God Our Help in Ages Past' was sung by all present.

The 'war to end all wars' ended on 11 November 1918. The townspeople gathered in The Square to celebrate peace and great numbers of flags were hung from all the shop windows. Of those men who had gone off to fight from Seaton, there were many who did not return. Those who did return found a changed England with signs that the insular life of Seaton was coming to an end. Following a public meeting, it was decided that a fitting memorial should be erected to the men of Seaton who had laid down their lives for their country. The site chosen was Seaton churchyard and the unveiling ceremony took place on Sunday 13 November 1921. At this touching ceremony, Mr Edward Cazelet Meade of Thornfield, on behalf of the townsfolk, asked Mr Clifford Gould, chairman of the Seaton Urban District Council, to unveil the cross. The vicar, Revd R.S. Robinson, then dedicated the memorial in loving memory of the following men:

Francis L.G. Akerman	Reginald W. Gosney
Reginald T. Hooper	William G. Oldridge
Colin Allardyce	William G. Gush
Percy Inge	Arthur P. Palmer
Harry Allardyce	Reginald P. Gigg
William Jones	William Perry
Percy C. Ball	Sidney F. Gigg
Reginald Mortimer	William G. Real
William Carslake	Alfred J. Green
Walter N. Newton	Richard C. Sutton
George Carslake	Charles W. Groves
James H. Newton	Charles C. Trineman
Alfred L. Dommett	Cyril Holmes
George T. Northcott	Eugene Trevett
Thomas Fry	William Haymes
Arthur J. Northcott	Robert White

Chapter 8

BETWEEN THE WARS: 1919–39

The war was now over and, along with the rest of the country, Seaton moved into the 'gay twenties'. It was during the 1920s that the motor car came into its own with local garages such as the Portman, opposite the Pole Arms, catering for their needs. The Portman was owned by Edgar Smith and he was also the local agent for Austin and Citroën cars. The well-known Ben Trevett had a garage in Station Road – he was the agent for Ford cars – and after his death in the 1940s his son, George, continued the business until the 1970s. Another well-known Seaton businessman was Arthur Good. His garage was also in Station Road. He advertised a daily service to Lyme Regis and Sidmouth by charabanc.

One of the most revolutionary changes after the First World War was the coming of the motor bus. Arthur Good was one of the pioneers of this new service and his chara-bancs feature in many of the photographs taken during this period, of parties about to

A Morris-Cowley for sixpence. Mr H.A. Good, with the car he won for sixpence at a fête held at Clinton's seat, Bicton, Devon.

embark on a trip to one of the local beauty spots. When you look at these photographs, the hood on the vehicle is always down – was this to help the photographer or did the sun always shine then? Maybe our grandparents were so hardy that they were impervious to the weather.

The General Strike in May 1926 brought the wheels of industry to a halt in the country for nine days and was the greatest concerted national strike ever seen in Great Britain. Repercussions were echoed in Seaton when, at a council meeting on 19 May 1926, a hearty vote of thanks on behalf of the town was given by the Chairman, C.C. Gould, to those ladies and gentlemen who had so readily come forward to assist during the period of the strike.

Practically every car owner had offered the use of his or her vehicle and many others, of all classes, had enrolled themselves as volunteers. In addition to the ladies who had given their services in connection with the Volunteer Service Committee, the mail had been transported in cars and the schoolchildren in Seaton had been taken to Colyton Grammar School.

Although the General Strike was long over by July it still affected Seaton, and at a council meeting that month, the clerk reported that the stock of coal in Seaton was rapidly diminishing and the amounts for which permits were given would have to be restricted. He asked members' opinions as to whether he should issue permits to the owners of the fair-roundabout who would shortly visit the town. After some discussion it was agreed that coal should not be supplied to the roundabout proprietor and that they should be informed that supplies in Seaton were not available. The coal shortage was due, despite the TUC calling off the strike unconditionally, to the miners staying out on strike until November. They were sold out and in the end were forced to return to work on the employers' terms.

The 1920s saw the introduction of the radio. The earliest sets were crystal sets which required very careful tuning – the crystal required touching in a sensitive spot with a piece of wire called 'the cat's whisker'. Later wireless sets were improved by valves. These replaced the crystal, allowing the signal to be amplified and doing away with the headphones. The first wireless engineer and dealer in Seaton was William Crawford, who lived in Beer Road. He was later to become the manager of the new Regal Cinema.

BOATING & FISHING

Above: *Seaton fishermen, 1925. Before the 1920s Seaton fishermen caught mackerel and herring in shoals. They kept the large boats which were rowed by four men with a net in each boat. The nets were pulled on to the beach with the catches of thousands of fish. However, by 1925 the local fishing industry was already fading, partly due to the sudden disappearance of the herring, the main source of income in the winter. In this picture are members of the well-known local fishing families of Newton and Wilkins.*

Above: *Herring catch, Seaton Beach, c.1923. Fisherman Nobby Snell is pictured here second from left. He played rugby for Devon and became a first reserve for England.*

Left: *The Newton family. For over 100 years the Newton family were fishermen on Seaton Beach. Family members pose in this picture with Dick Wilkins (second from left). A wonder character, he was one of the best-known men on the beach until his death in the 1970s. Tom Newton (second from right), won the BEM during the Second World War when he pushed a mine out of the River Axe with an oar.*

Right: *The wooden schooner* Malpas Belle *(shown in photograph as brigantine rig), 179 gross tons, 109.2' x 22.7' s 12.1', built 1872 by Nicholas Scoble, Malpas, Truro. The boat became stranded in heavy weather and went to pieces on Seaton Beach, 3 February 1922, during a voyage from Antwerp to Penarth, with a cargo of bog ore on board.*

Left: *Seaton regatta day, c.1925. Regatta day was held on the last Thursday in July and was the major event of East Devon. All the showmen, such as Anderton and Rowlands, Hancocks and Brewers, brought their fairs and other entertainers flocked to the town.*

Axmouth Harbour, 1925. The long narrow building was once an old warehouse. Before the coming of the railway, Axmouth Harbour was very busy and a place of no little importance. But by the time of this photograph it had become a quiet backwater. The Stedcombe estate sold the harbour to Axminster RDC in 1967, ownership passing to East Devon District Council in 1974.

LOCAL VIEWS

Above: *Marine Place, c.1924.*
The drinking fountain to the right
of the foreground was given to
the town by Mr and Mrs Willans
to mark the Diamond Jubilee of
Queen Victoria in 1897.

Right: *High tide combined with*
strong winds caused foam to be
blown over Seaton seafront, 1930.

Sea Hill, 1926. The wall one can see on the
right was the boundary wall of Seafield
House destroyed by enemy action
during the Second World War.

Below: *Marlpit Lane, c.1923. In those days it was known as Lovers Lane to the locals.*

Above: *Seatonians haymaking, 1928. This photograph was taken in Lakes Field. This is now the site of houses on the north side of Highwell Road to the old back entrance to Ryalls Court. From left to right: Jack Lake, John Gosling, Bill Whatley, John Pengelley.*

Looking up Queen Street, 1925. At the time of this photograph S. Lock Esq. had a bakers and confectioners business in the corner building now occupied by the George Inn. On the opposite side, Abbots sold fancy gifts, tobacco and high-class stationery.

By the 1930s, the Radio House in Seaton had a full range of the new HMV wireless sets, including the all-electric and the battery type. The top of the range was the fluid-light, five valve, mains supernet which sold for 13½ guineas.

In the present age it is difficult to imagine the difference the radio made. In the 1920s, the wireless had been a cross between a scientific toy and a miracle, but by 1932, when the King broadcast to the Empire on Christmas Day, the miracle was taken for granted and in most homes families grouped together to listen to the wireless set.

The first regular cinema shows were in the Town Hall, which screened films every Thursday and Saturday – they advertised 'the steadiest and best pictures in the district'. Of course in those days they were silent films – the 'talkies' arriving in Seaton in 1929 with 'The Jazz Singer', starring Al Jolson.

The secretary of the Town Hall Company at this time was William George White, who must have led a busy life because he was also the secretary of the Town Social Club in Station Road. The social club provided its members with a billiards room and games room; there was also a reading room. The annual subscription in those days was 7s.6d. The club is still going strong today and at the end of the century had been running for 80 years – a remarkable achievement, with credit due to all concerned for providing so much pleasure for countless thousands of Seatonians.

A list of clubs, societies and organisations which then existed in the town would have included the Seaton Bowling Club, who were playing on rinks in Colyford Road, a Miniature Rifle Club, the Lawn Tennis and Cricket Club, the Axe Cliff Golf Club, a Football Club and the Seaton and District Choral Society.

The Choral Society was formed on 24 January 1924 when Mr C.C. Gould chaired a meeting of over 40 people. It was decided to perform Coleridge Taylor's *Hiawa'tha's Wedding Feast*. This was to be the first of many successful productions throughout the 1920s, conducted by the well-loved William Walton. He could draw on the talents of fine local singers such as Norah Gould, Mary Gunn, Harry Clapp, Arthur Smart, Bertram Bartlett and the Misses Lansdown.

Going back to football, in those days Seaton was divided into two – the part of town north of Manor Road was called Rags Alley, and if you were a lad at that time you played football for either Rags Alley or The Town. The pitch was always the Cliff Field – now the turf of the bowling green – and the rivalry was keen.

One of the most important events to take place during the 1920s was the opening of the new West Walk. The old West Walk was washed away during a storm in 1915 and was replaced by the present walk in 1924. The coping-stone was laid by the chairman of Seaton Urban District Council, Mr C.C. Gould, in 1924, and at a later date the West Walk was officially opened by Morrison Bell, the local MP.

Seaton and Colyton Operatic Society at Seaton Town Hall, 1920.

The funeral cortège of James Leyman, the builder responsible for the Highwell Road development, pictured in Highwell Road, 1925.

Left: *Seaton bell-ringers, 15 August 1937. Left to right, back row: F.R. Brown, F. Abbott, A.H. Bradford; middle row: A. Gigg, T.O. Hilder; front row: J. Board, W.B. Boundy (Capt.), G. Northcott.*

Below: *Tea in the hayfield at Couchill Farm – taken during the 1930s. Left to right: ? Thomas, Ernest Wilson, Thomas senr, ? Carslake and ? Thomas.*

SEATON AS RESORT

Above: *Seaton Esplanade, 1925.*

Right: *White Cliff, Seaton, c.1925.*
The path in the foreground went down to the
beach at Seaton Hole to the west of Seaforth Lodge
on the old Beer road. The path was in use until
the 1940s when it fell away during a wet winter.

Guests and staff of the Cliff Hotel in fancy dress, 1923.

Above: *The cliff path to Seaton Hole, 1924.*

Holiday-makers 1930s style, Seaton Esplanade.

Right: *Opening of the West Walk, 1925. The old West Walk was washed away during a storm in 1915 and was replaced by the present walk in 1924. The coping-stone was laid by the chairman of Seaton Urban District Council, Mr C.C. Gould, in 1924, and at a later date the West Walk was officially opened by Morrison Bell, the local MP seen here cutting the ribbon.*

Left: *The new West Walk looking east, 1927.*

The West Walk seen just after it was opened in 1925.

The Chine, 1927. Built in the 1920s as an extension of the West Walk this proved to be a valuable asset to the town.

The East Walk, 1926. The fine building on the left was then the splendid Beach Hotel.

Seaton Beach, 1927.

Seaton Esplanade looking west, c.1925. The attractive building to the right of the foreground was the Westleigh Hotel. Built by George Henry Richards, the Westleigh was one of seven hotels in the town, which have all now ceased trading. The house standing in the present Jubilee Gardens was called Seafield. This was destroyed by a German bomber during the Second World War.

The Westleigh Hotel, 1925.

LOCAL BODIES & AMENITIES

Above: *The first public electricity came to Seaton in the 1920s with the Seaton and District Electric Light Company. The power station was in Homer Lane and pictured outside these premises are Bill Sutton (left) who remained with the company after it became SWEB and Teddy Haslop (right) who later began his own electricity business.*

Right: *The main office of the Seaton and District Electric Light Company, c.1929, now occupied by C.M.C. Financial Advisers.*

Smiths Lending Library, Fore Street, c.1923. W. Smith Esq., who was a printer, ran a successful lending library and fancy goods shop situated on the present site of Maynews.

It was about the same time that the first public electricity supply came to Seaton. The formation of the Seaton and District Electric Light Company heralded a new era for the town, bringing light and heat at the turn of a switch. The directors of this new venture were Brig.-General G.B. Smith, Charles Gane, A. Morton Dovey, Major-General H.B.H. Wright and Stanley Cooper. The chief engineer was Mr P.O. Witty and the power station was in Homer Lane, in a building which is occupied by the Christian Cross Road Centre at the time of writing.

It was in 1935 that the Seaton Electricity Company held an exhibition in the Town Hall. Visitors, who were used to gas lighting and coal fires, came away impressed by the efficiency and cleanliness of electricity in the home and the observation was made that 'if the Seaton district does not in consequence become more electrically minded in the future, we shall be very much surprised.'

By 1929 the old social order was only a shadow of its former self. Things were changing and in that year the Labour Party was returned to Government for the first time in history. Also for the first time, a woman became a minister – Margaret Bondfield, who was born in Chard and knew Seaton well, became Minister of Labour.

Unfortunately the new Labour Government proved to be as ineffectual as the Conservatives in stemming the rise of unemployment and by 1932 there were nearly three million people on the dole. Despite this, the people of Seaton remained happy. They appear to have missed the tides of depression that were sweeping the country and local errand boys could be heard whistling tunes such as 'On the Sunny Side of the Street', 'Happy Days are Here Again' and the immortal 'Life is Just a Bowl of Cherries'. Strange as it may seem, in those days of the dole and the means test, these were the country's most popular songs.

The post-First World War period saw the continuing growth of Seaton as a holiday resort and, by the 1930s, as a retirement area. The Mitchell Brothers, whose first office adjoined the Town Hall, were responsible for building most of Fremington Road and Durley Road, Newlands Park, Greenways and the west side of Castle Hill during this period. Other builders included K.F. Mottram who built many of the fine houses in New Beer Road, and Arthur Turner who, with his sons, developed Harepath Road and Court Lane.

During the 1930s, Burnham's *Seaton Guide* provided would-be holiday-makers with a list of local accommodation available in guest-houses and apartments. One of those who advertised was a Miss Dauncey who lived in Manor Road. The following letter was written by her in July 1930, in answer to an enquiry:

Dear Sir, I can take you July 26 provided you are all strong, healthy people. I do not take anyone suffering from any infections. The little bedroom is mine and I sleep in the box-room in order to let it. I do not take dogs or anyone disfigured or without an arm or leg. I am ever so sorry for the latter but cannot bear to see them about the house. You would have a cold lunch and a late dinner at 7.30, would you not? That is the only way I can manage a large party; it gives me time to clean up and prepare for dinner. My terms are five guineas for the best three rooms and one guinea for the single bedroom; five guineas the first week, six guineas the next two weeks; sixpence each hot bath, and you must not have too many of them as I have to watch the geyser 20 minutes. I dare say you bathe in the sea and you can have hot water. I also make a small charge for cruet unless you care to find your own. I am a good cook and if you come, will do all I can to make you comfortable. Please answer my questions with regard to invalids, etc.

Miss Dauncey, who died in the 1950s, was a local eccentric character, well known to old Seatonians. The sentiments expressed in her reply would not be acceptable in these days of political correctness. In those days Seaton, like so many small West Country towns, had many characters – ready in speech, wise in the craft of the land and suspicious of strangers.

Great excitement was felt by all in the town when, in 1934, Captain Harry Warner announced plans to build a holiday camp in Seaton. Most business people welcomed the news, expecting a spin-off from this new breed of visitor. This expectation did materialise, with many shops becoming dependent on the campers.

For working-class people the seaside was still a place to dream about. Less than three million workers had paid holidays and it was not until 1938 that the Parliament Bill for all industrial workers to have a week's paid holiday became law. It was then that holiday camps became a ray of sunshine in a dreary, drab world, allowing members of the working class to have a week's holiday for a week's pay. Although holiday camps were not a new idea in England, the vision that Captain Warner had for his Seaton venture was different; it really was the first 'hi-de-hi' camp – indeed Billy Butlin was then on the board of the Warner company.

The camp took only three months to build and it opened at Easter 1936 for 200 people. The men who built the Warner camp formed the nucleus of the team who, a few months later, were to build the first Butlins camp at Skegness.

Warners at Seaton was a family camp for mum, dad and the children. For the next 50 years, until it changed to Haven Holiday Village, it provided holidays for thousands of people. They took part in entertainment programmes which included 'glamorous granny' and 'knobbly knees' competitions, and would return home with fond recollections

Above: *Presentation and dedication of first converted ambulance in Seaton, 1938–39, with Superintendant Moore of Axminster taking the salute.*

Below right: *Clifford Charles Gould was born on 23 April 1866 and in 1895 became one of the first members of the newly formed Seaton Urban District Council. In 1916 he became the council chairman, a position he held until his death in 1939. He was an outstanding figure in the public life of Seaton for over 40 years, a man who lived for the town.*

Above: *The St John's Ambulance men, seen here looking very smart, were attending the dedication of the first motor ambulance in Seaton, c.1938. Originally a Chrysler car belonging to Dr James of the Ryalls Court School, it was given to the town and converted to an ambulance by A. Dowell & Sons, coach builders, of Exeter. Mr H.F. Norcombe, the wartime chairman of Seaton Council, is seen standing on the left next to Harry Clapp. The three St John's Ambulance men standing against the vehicle were,* left to right: *Mr Barr, Mr A. Gapper and Mr C. Minhinnett.*

DAYS OF CELEBRATION

Right: *Cliff Castle floodlit during the Silver Jubilee week of King George V, May 1935. The original photograph was entered in the Amateur Photographer Silver Jubilee competition. It was taken with an Ilford plate camera. Time exposure was half an hour.*

Street decorations in Fore Street for the Silver Jubilee of George V, 1935.

Decorations in The Square for the Silver Jubilee of George V, 1935.

Girl Guides parade for King George V's Silver Jubilee day on Seaton's seafront, 1935.

A Seaton wedding, 1934. Left to right: *Revd Robinson (vicar of St Gregory's), Mr Stone (father of the bridegroom), Mr L. Stone (bridegroom), Miss Kathleen Hooper (bride), Mr Donald Hooper, Miss Peggy Stone, Mr John Stone; ?; sitting in front, left to right: Mrs Julia Hooper (mother of bride), Mrs Stone (mother of bridegroom).*

SPORT

Seaton Football Club was formed in 1919 and this historic photograph shows the very first team assembled outside the George Inn to have their picture taken with local supporters. Left to right, standing, back row: Walt Ware, ? Douglas (goal), Cyril Watts; middle row: Fred Osborne, Les Northcott, Barr Snell; front: Will Akerman, Ralph Rogers, Frank Miller, Jo Collins, Harry Gibbens.

Seaton football team, 1924.

Above: *Seaton Miniature Golf Links on Cliff Field, c.1927.*

Left: *Mr C.C. Gould,* (on the right), *is seen opening the 1934 season of Seaton Bowling Club.*

Right: *Riding lessons at Ryalls Court School, c.1933.*

Members of Seaton Bowling Club, c.1935.

of Seaton, with memories to treasure for the rest of their lives.

The camp was to play a major part in the economy of the town, providing much-needed jobs for local people – also helping the cashflow into the tills of local shops. Some people would try to play down the importance of the camp, stating that it contributed little or nothing to the town's economy. Seaton, however, should be proud of a centre where the staff were devoted to making sure that people enjoyed themselves and had the holiday of their lives at a modest cost. Captain Warner had that rare gift, also possessed by Billy Butlin – the 'common touch'. They knew what people wanted and made sure they got it.

Not long after the holiday camp opened, Seaton got its own purpose-built cinema, The Regal, in Fore Street. Local people thought The Regal was the height of luxury, where sixpence would buy three hours of entertainment in a soft seat in plush surroundings. You could have tea in the tea lounge or buy a bag of sweets and a bar of chocolate in the foyer kiosk. The cinema became a place to escape from the ever-threatening real world outside. How many locals can remember the 6ft 3in smart green-uniformed commissionaire, Mr Bland, and his little wife who was an usherette – nicknamed by all the young boys as 'King Kong' and 'Minnie Mouse'?

It was during the 1930s that many of the older generation who had wielded influence in the town passed away, to be replaced by men of the new generation. Seaton's leading citizen, Mr C.C. Gould, Chairman of Seaton Urban District Council for over 25 years, died in 1938 and local doctor, Edward Tonge, died in 1937. Others to leave the scene included George Barton, the town's photographer who had recorded so many events in Seaton in a 40-year stint, local vicar Revd R.S. Robinson, Thomas Clapp, founder of Clapps Transport, Mr C.F. Gosney the chemist, Arthur Perry the artist, Edward Cazelet Meade of Thornfield and F. Scargill Esq. They had all left their mark on the town's history. Change is natural and one man's dusk becomes another man's dawn. New men like Frank Norcombe and Ben Turner appeared, who were to guide the town in new directions in future years. They were joined by people like Teddy Haslop, George Trevett, Geoffrey Clapp, Percy Litton, Howard Bayliss, Charles Taylor, Arch Richards, Jim Smith, John Webby and many others who, like them, helped the people of Seaton to face the troubled times that lay ahead.

The era that had commenced with the depression of 1930 ended in 1939 with war. Following the short period of relief felt by the country in 1938, when Prime Minister Chamberlain returned home from his meeting at Munich with Hitler declaring 'peace in our time', came the realisation in 1939 that war was inevitable.

Revd R.S. Robinson is pictured here passing Seafield Terrace driving an open touring car and heading the local church parade, c.1927.

Just before the outbreak of war, young men from Seaton, Beer and Branscombe were attending the summer camp of the 4th Battalion Devonshire Regiment (Territorials) at Corfe. They were volunteers and these summer training camps were a chance to enjoy a break from everyday life together with local friends. They were to return home to witness the illusions of the 1930s finally disappear when, with the people of Seaton, they heard Mr Chamberlain speaking over the radio, saying in a strained voice that we were at war with Germany.

One of the first incidents of the Second World War occurred on Sunday 17 September 1939 when the aircraft-carrier HMS *Courageous* was sunk by a German U-boat (U29) in the Atlantic, to the west of Ireland. A total of 519 of her crew perished, including Captain W.T. Makeig Jones of Seaton. John Wells from Seaton, who had joined the Navy as a boy seaman in 1938, was also serving on the *Courageous* and escaped by climbing through a porthole. Shortly after his escape, John Wells paid a visit to his old Seaton school, 'Sir Walter Trevelyan's' where, after he had been introduced by the headmaster, John Webby, he related his experience to the enthralled pupils.

Warners Holiday Camp was requisitioned and re-opened in October 1939 as an internment camp for classified aliens. A high barbed-wire fence was erected around the camp and the guards included local Territorials. Many of these internees were to die during the spring of 1940 when they were deported to Canada on the pre-war luxury liner, *The Andorra Star*. This liner was torpedoed and sunk by a German U-boat in the Atlantic.

One of the internees was the famous anti-Nazi lawyer and journalist, Sebastian Haffner. He stayed at the Warner Holiday Camp until April 1940 when he was released after representations were made to the Home Office. Haffner remained in London, working for the *Observer* newspaper until 1954. He then went back to Germany and wrote for *Die Welt* and for *Stern* magazine. He was the author of several historial best-sellers, including *The Rise and Fall of Prussia*, *From Bismark to Hitler* and *The Meaning of Hitler*, which sold nearly one million copies. He died in 1999, aged 91.

A manuscript found by Haffner's son after his death was recently published in a book, *Defying Hitler*. It is said that no other book has ever explained so clearly how it was possible for the Nazis to gain a foothold and make a whole nation into a pack of hunting hounds, directed against humans.

Shortly after the outbreak of war, long lines of children could be seen in the cities making their way to the railway station for evacuation to the country. Over a four-day period, 4,000 trains were used to transport more than 1,300,000 evacuees. This was a remarkable undertaking and much credit was due to the organisers. The evacuees who arrived in Seaton would have been met by Mr Brewer, the Billeting Officer, who had the unenviable job of placing the

Passengers leave the Clarence Hotel (now the sports shop)
for a day-trip in a Lancia open-top coach, c.1926.

children into suitable homes. Mainly due to the organising ability of Mr Brewer, most of the evacuees settled into their new homes quite quickly; indeed, many of them were to remain in Seaton for the rest of their lives.

The first months of the Second World War became known as 'the phoney war'. This ended in April 1940 with the invasions of Holland and Denmark. Disaster followed disaster and after Dunkirk, Britain stood alone. It was then that the people of Seaton became united as never before – or, indeed, since. Churchill had made that magnificent speech, '... we shall fight them on the beaches...', and, in response, on a hot weekend in June, everyone in the town, from the very young to the very old, assembled on Seaton Beach to dig a trench as a first defence against the threatened invasion. This, indeed, was their finest hour.

In 1840, Seaton was a community of 765 people who were almost cut off from the outside world. Since that date, waves of change had broken over this Devon town. Although its contribution to national events had been minimal, occasionally distant rumbles from the outside world had been heard. However, it was not until 1940 that the people of Seaton faced a major threat; they were ready; they had come of age.

Clapps Seaton bus, 1930.

Mr Gould's staff and friends coach outing to Dartmoor, 1929. This group of Seatonians includes Mr J. Gosling, Mr Gould, Mr Pengelly, Mr Hutchings, the Misses Needs and the coach driver, Jack Spurway.

THE OPEN ROAD

*The steamroller seen here was engaged on road repairs on the Colyford Road, c.1930.
The man with the horse and cart was the late Bill Whatley.*

*Trevetts Garage, Harbour Road, Seaton, c.1937. Trevetts Garage traded successfully for over
60 years until the 1970s. Staff pictured here, left to right: Ralph Anning, Stanley Parker,
Alex Parr, Horace Clark (foreman), Dick Iles and Bert Williams.*

Left: *Couchill Hill Climb, 1936. Couchill was a popular venue for motorcycling events which included hill climbs and scrambles from the late 1920s until just after the Second World War.*

Right: *Construction of the new road to Axmouth from Axe Bridge, 1924.*

The Seaton to Beer bus, 1929.

Tar spraying to re-grit the road outside the Kings Arms, 1935.

Walt Peach, c.1938. The carthorse pictured here, well groomed with shining brasses, belonged to Seaton Urban District Council where Mr Peach was employed for many years.

Inset: *Gun emplacement in Cliff Field above the West Walk, Seaton, c.1942. Built to resemble a house, it provided camouflage for two 6" guns which were used for coastal defence. They fired 100lb shells and during one early gun practice, the noise from the barrage shattered windows in nearby houses.*

Above: *This bomb crater is all that was left when German hit-and-run raiders dropped bombs on Seafield House on 26 October 1942. This is now the site of Jubilee Gardens.*

Members of the Seaton Observer Corps at their post in Seaton, c.1943.

Chapter 9

THE SECOND WORLD WAR: 1940–45

By the beginning of June, most of western Europe had fallen to the might of the well-equipped and well-trained German army. Many people thought that we had lost the war when suddenly, with a force and language, Churchill, with his ornate phraseology and his instinctive feel for Britain's glorious past, made millions dare to hope again. People in Seaton who were alive at that time will well remember his speeches on the radio which made listeners feel a part of that glorious time in history. His voice sent shivers down the spine and few will ever forget that experience.

In Seaton, voluntary services were quickly organised for the national emergency and when an appeal broadcast for recruits to the Local Defence Volunteers was made, it was met with an immediate response. The name was soon changed to the Home Guard (although they were always known affectionately as Dad's Army). These men from Seaton played an important part in the Second World War and, after their final muster in 1945, much appreciation was felt by all for the voluntary work they had done during the difficult days of the war. The Observer Corps were formed and from their look-out post on Clay Common they kept continuous watch, day and night, reporting all aircraft movement.

At the outbreak of war there were more than 1,400 local fire authorities in England and Wales and these were consolidated into a single national fire service, giving the advantages of greater mobility and a universal standard of training and equipment. The skilful dedication of the Seaton National Fire Service must never be forgotten; they played an heroic part in the defence of Exeter against enemy bombing and were at hand when hit-and-run raiders dropped bombs on Seaton.

Seaton was fortunate at that time to have a vicar who knew the horrors of war first-hand. Revd Harry Cooke had won the Military Cross in the First World War and was a natural leader of men. His wife, Norah, was also a war heroine in her own right, having served as a VAD nurse and survived the sinking of the hospital ship, *Britannic*, in the Gulf of Athens in November 1916.

Revd Cooke led the town in many of the national days of prayer; he was, with his Christian faith, a source of comfort to many people in Seaton during those difficult times. Revd Cooke was a man dedicated to Seaton and the Christian faith.

In October 1940, 150 more evacuees from the East End of London arrived at 12 hours' notice. Once again Mr Brewer, assisted by members of voluntary organisations, achieved wonders. One of the evacuees was a young Terry Scales who came from South London. His first shock was trying to understand the speech pattern as the locals seemed to converse with strange words such as 'dasn't', 'casn't', 'thake', closer to James I's English than the language he was familiar with. His years in Seaton were one long adventure and probably the most significant single experience in his life. Being so closely in touch with nature sowed the seeds of his future career – that of a landscape painter.

Programme for the Wings for Victory Week, 22–29 May 1943.

Other evacuees included the Baker family, the Pritchards, Soapy Hudson and his sister, Jim Thomas, Alfie Gillett and his sister, and many others.

The chairman of Seaton Urban District Council during the war years was Frank Norcombe. He was probably the most able council chairman that the town ever had and proved to be the right man for the job.

By the end of 1940, strict food rationing was introduced and people were encouraged to 'dig for victory' by growing their own food in their gardens and allotments. Blackout material was in great demand to cover the windows at night and strict control was exercised on householders by the ARP and special constabulary. The people of Seaton were provided with identity cards and petrol was strictly rationed through coupons for the few vehicles allowed on the road. Vehicles could only obtain their petrol from a few designated garages; the only garage in the area allowed to sell petrol was Trevetts in Station Road.

Throughout the war years, a most charming and gentle priest, Father Ortiz from Portugal, served at St Augustine's Catholic Church in Manor Road. He spoke very little English but was much loved by all for his sympathy for the British in our time of danger. The Catholic community in Seaton at that time was quite small but the Gospel Hall attracted many stalwart worshippers who were led in prayer by Mr A.S. Ferris and Mr Ben Turner. The war years brought the followers of all the town's religions closer together, showing a tolerance towards each other.

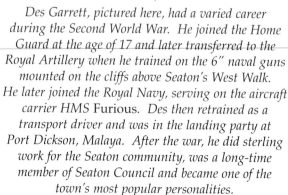

*Des Garrett, pictured here, had a varied career during the Second World War. He joined the Home Guard at the age of 17 and later transferred to the Royal Artillery when he trained on the 6" naval guns mounted on the cliffs above Seaton's West Walk.
He later joined the Royal Navy, serving on the aircraft carrier HMS Furious. Des then retrained as a transport driver and was in the landing party at Port Dickson, Malaya. After the war, he did sterling work for the Seaton community, was a long-time member of Seaton Council and became one of the town's most popular personalities.*

*Troop Leader Ronald Anning and Patrol Leader William Green, pictured here during August 1943, are wearing their Scout gilt crosses which had been presented to them for gallantry by Colonel O'Donnell, the assistant county commissioner, at a ceremony in the Church Institute, Seaton. They were on the opposite side of the River Axe when they noticed that 12-year-old Connie Wall had entered the water and got into difficulties.
This girl was half way across and had gone down twice by the time they reached her. They succeeded in getting her to the side of the river and this plucky rescue saved the girl from drowning.*

Seaton Scout Bank, Cross Street, Seaton, c.1943. The band was playing for the opening ceremony of the Seaton, Colyton, Beer and District Wings for Victory Week on Saturday 22 May 1943. The target for the week was £50,000 which would have bought one bomber and two Typhoons. Standing to the left of the band is Scoutmaster Skipper Brooks.

CHRISTMAS GREETINGS
AND BEST WISHES
FROM
THE PEOPLE OF SEATON

Christmas card sent to serving members of the Armed Forces during the Second World War from the people of Seaton.

Presentation to the Czech Army, 1943. Frank Norcombe, chairman of Seaton Urban District Council, is seen here attaching a ribbon to the colours of the 2nd Battalion Czech Army at Dover Court near Harwich.

Czechoslovak Army Concert:
given

ON SATURDAY, JULY 11th - 8,30 p.m.

P R O G R A M M E

CZECHOSLOVAK ARMY CHOIR
        Festivity Song .... B.Smetana
INTRODUCTORY REMARKS .... Lft.F.
Czechoslovak Army Choir
        If I were a little bird .... Schneider-Trnavský
        Old Tower of Trenčín .... Slovak Folk Song
        To the Devil wi' you,lads....... Slovak Folk Song
TENOR SOLOS - CAPTAIN J.VALEK
        Cloves and Roses .... Czech Folk Song
        Why hurry to marry .... Slovak Folk Song
        English song
        Flower song , Carmen .... G.Bizet

CZECHOSLOVAK CAMP BAND

I N T E R V A L

Czechoslovak Army Choir
        The village bells .... A.Dvořák
        The Banquet .... A.Dvořák
        Into Battle .... J.Zajc
        My precious Johnny .... F.Vránek
        The Bartered Bride, by Smetana,Arie Kecala
        Baso Růžička

Czechoslovak Camp Band

oooooooo

NATIONAL ANTHEMS
oooooooo

CZECHOSLOVAK ARMY CHOIR arranged and conducted by Lt.J.OBRUČA
CAMP BAND arranged and conducted by Sgt.M.MARTIN
PIANO Accompanist : Sgt. M.MARTIN

Organised by the Information Department of the CZECHOSLOVAK
ARMY in conjunction with the LOCAL RED CROSS
oooooooo

OPEN AIR CONCERT will be held in front of the ESPLANADE HOTEL
6 - 7 p.m.
oooooooo

Programme for the concert given by the Czechoslovakian Army on Saturday 11 July 1942.

The Bomb Disposal Squad seen here are winching an unexploded bomb from Mrs Irene Fox's garden at Westmead, Seaton Down Road, 1944. The 1,000lb bomb came from a German aircraft that was being chased out to sea; to facilitate its escape it had jettisoned its load of two 1,000lb bombs.

The staff of the Pole Arms Hotel in the garden during the wartime Christmas of 1944.
Left to right: The well-known Nippy Ball (saddler and barman), Gladys (waitress),
George (postman), Mrs Meyer (the licensee's wife), Hetty (chambermaid),
Peacy (cellarman), Ivy (chambermaid), Bill (gardener).

By the end of 1940, the flood of evacuees to Seaton was so great that the main school, Sir Walter Trevelyan, could not cope and other centres, like the Congregational Hall in Cross Street and the church rooms on the Colyford Road, were commandeered. John Webby was then the much-loved headmaster of Trevelyan School. He was a teacher of outstanding ability and a perfect disciplinarian – when boys were ordered to the front of his class for punishment, they knew they deserved all they would get.

During the period from August 1940 to 1943, East Devon was subjected to many air raids. Seaton was the target for hit-and-run German raiders who were attempting to destroy the naval gun on Cliff Field, which was disguised as a small house. Unfortunately, another house nearby, at the corner of Seahill and Castle Hill, was hit and demolished, resulting in the death of Major Cartwright and his family who were having lunch at the time.

Other bombs fell in Highwell Road and Harepath Road where Mrs Walton, widow of the church organist, and two evacuee girls were killed. As a protection against these sudden air raids, an air-raid shelter was built beside the Church of the Good Shepherd for the use of the townspeople.

Special war savings weeks were held at intervals in Seaton between 1941 and 1945. These comprised War Weapons Week, Warship Week, Wings for Victory Week and Salute the Soldier Week.

Victory celebrations, Highwell Road, c.1945.
This street party was held to celebrate victory in Europe.
Standing on the left is the Seaton vicar, Revd H.R. Cooke
MC, who would have paid a visit to the many street
parties held on that day.

There are few reminders in present-day Seaton of the many thousands of troops who were stationed in the town between 1940–45. Amongst them were French Canadians, units of the Free Polish and Czechoslovakian Army, the Free Spanish Army and, of course, much to the delight of the local girls, the American troops.

The Czechoslovakian Army were remembered when Frank Norcombe, Chairman of Seaton Urban District Council, and Francis Garner, Clerk to the Council, visited Dovercourt near Harwich, accompanied by their wives, in 1943. On this occasion Frank Norcombe attached a ribbon to the colours of the 2nd Battalion of the Czech Army who were stationed at Seaton for part of the war. Some of the Czechs returned to Seaton after the war for a visit and were able to renew their acquaintance with Frank.

As D-Day approached, the area became very active as American troops were dispersed in the surrounding country lanes and woods. When the great day came, all the troops suddenly disappeared overnight.

Following the landings on the Normandy beaches, a tank landing craft, *HM LCT 1137*, suffered damage on D-Day on those beaches and broke its back on the return journey. Crew members managed to secure the broken halves with chains but navigation proved difficult, and instead of returning to its base at Portland it ended up on Seaton Beach. It stayed there – much to the delight of the local boys – until the 1950s!

Although the sea front was still barricaded with barbed wire and concrete 'tank trap' pyramids, the threat of invasion was over and no more air-raid alerts were sounded. Every day brought more news of the liberation of Europe until, finally, the day of victory arrived. Further names were to be added to the list of those who had been killed in the First World War to remind future generations, once again, of the cost of war.

At long last on 8 May 1945 peace in Europe came and a two-day holiday was declared. Free entertainment, communal lunches and tea parties were held in the streets of Seaton. In Britain's time-honoured way of signalling victory since the Armada, massive bonfires were lit on prominent sites and a tremendous feeling of relief spread over Seaton and the whole of East Devon.

The instrument of unconditional surrender was signed on 7 May 1945 to take place on the 8th. During the evening of 7 May, patrons of the Royal Cinema, Seaton, stood up and cheered when the cinema lights went up at 9.00p.m. and an emotion-filled Mr Crawford, the cinema manager, announced that war with Germany was over. This, indeed, must have been the proudest moment of his life.

Chapter 10

TOWARDS 2000

By the end of the war, the spirit of the nation had changed; no one in 1945 wanted to go back to 1939. With the slogan 'Victory at all costs', the British people had won and were now fully confident to go forwards, into the future.

The General Election that took place on 5 July swept the Labour Party into power. The Conservatives had relied on the glory of Churchill's name but the Labour Party offered a programme for the future. Even so, East Devon, with Seaton, remained true blue and Cedric Drewe kept this seat for the Conservatives, but by the late afternoon of 26 July, Clement Attlee was the new Prime Minister.

Much excitement was felt in the town when the Seaton Town Hall caught fire during the early hours of Sunday morning, 22 January 1945. A few hours after Saturday-night dancers had left the building, it was ablaze from end to end and all that was left of it on Sunday morning was a skeleton. Heroic efforts by the National Fire Service saved the front of the premises in Fore Street, including the Council Offices, Masonic Hall and Seaton branch of the County Library, and the caretaker's living quarters at the rear.

The dance concluded at midnight and the outbreak was discovered at about 4a.m. by Mr and Mrs French whose shop and residence adjoined the Town Hall. Mr French aroused the caretaker, Mr Bert Gifford, whose wife and daughter, Jacqueline, went to the Pole Arms Hotel, a few doors away, in their night attire. Mr French telephoned the fire brigade who quickly arrived on the scene, at the same time as PS Abrahams and PWR Gapper from the police station. By then the building was a raging inferno with black smoke pouring from the roof and flames leaping up to illuminate the whole centre of the town.

The Seaton Brigade were reinforced by units from Colyton, Axminster, Sidmouth and Honiton. In the charge of Company Officer Thorn, they obtained a plentiful supply of water from the fire hydrants and static water tanks and had seven or eight powerful jets in use. They concentrated their efforts on saving the buildings at either end of the main hall and succeeded, the only damage to these premises being caused by the water.

The fire was subdued by 5.30a.m. when all that was left of the Town Hall were the bare walls, roof, girders and charred beams. The slate roof had gone and the whole of the wooden floor, panelling around the walls, the stage and balcony had been reduced to cinders. A large number of chairs stored under the stage, two pianos on top and an amplifier belonging to the Red Cross were completely burnt. The Town Hall was rebuilt and reopened in 1952.

The dropping of the atomic bomb during August 1945 saw the end of the war with Japan. Once again, a two-day national holiday was declared with street parties held throughout the town. The church bells of St Gregory's rang out and the general rejoicings ended on the second night when the entire town gathered together on the sea front. During that evening, a Japanese prisoner of war who had returned early was present – a young soldier who was a member of the Rogers family. He was chair-lifted and carried shoulder-high through the cheering crowd. Once again the chairman of the council, Frank Norcombe, proved his worth in leading the town, not only in the joyous celebrations that took place but also in the Christian faith of thanksgiving.

In the immediate post-war period, the Seaton Branch British Legion played an important part in the town. They, in partnership with the Football Club, restarted the Seaton Carnival. Legion members also organised the Seaton Regatta and the Seaton Autumn Show. Bill Hatchley, the vice chairman of the branch, was the main mover and his early death in 1951 robbed the town of a very able organiser.

Members of Seaton Urban District Council attended a naming ceremony on 25 June 1946 at Seaton Junction when a locomotive, a Light Pacific of the West Country Class No. 21C 12V, was named *Seaton*. In 1968 its name-plate was presented to the Seaton Council who failed to appreciate its great monetary and historical value and, unfortunately, managed to lose it. Bearing in mind its size, this must have been quite difficult to do.

The Seaton railway branch line closed on 5 March 1966. It was a sad day for Seaton. Following the Beeching Plan, the closure of the line was proposed and, despite strong local objections, was confirmed by the Minister of Transport. After 98 years, the last round trip was on Saturday 5 March 1966 and the last train to leave Seaton, a DMV, was driven by Harold Pope.

FESTIVAL OF BRITAIN

The post-war gloom in Britain was temporarily lifted by the Festival of Britain. The central feature of this festival was the South Bank exhibition, on the South Bank of the Thames near Waterloo Station. It was an immediate success and people flocked to it in their thousands. The celebrations held nationwide were in commemoration of Prince Albert's Exhibition of 1851 and to demonstrate Britain's economic recovery. The Festival of Britain was opened by King George VI from the steps of St Paul's on 3 May 1951. Celebrations were held that day throughout East Devon and the author was the organising secretary of the day's events in Seaton. One of the highlights was the pyramid display given by the Youth Club on Seaton seafront. In the top picture we have the team, left to right: Derek Real, Derek Jones, Brian Steele, Alan Baker, Brian Davis, Edward Cockram, ?, Dick Moore, Don Rogers. In the lower picture, the team demonstrate one of the positions, watched by the admiring crowd.

LOCAL CHARACTERS & DIGNITARIES

Ben Welch, Seaton fisherman (left) *with brother Jack Welch, Seaton auctioneer,*
watching the world go by, sitting outside the old Seaton Library.

Above: *Ted Gosling with a 1928 vintage Singer 8 which he purchased for £4. The photograph was taken at the bottom of Eyewell Green in 1956.*

Right: *Well-known local character Bob Haynes who worked for Seaton Council for many years.*

Left: *Father Christmas makes a visit to Seaton's OAPs at a party in the Congregational Church in Cross Street, c.1960.*

Left: *Local dignitaries at a Rotary evening, c.1971.* Left to right: *Mr and Mrs Isgrove, ?, ?, Mr Chubb, Roy Chapple, Ann Clare.*

Below: *Mr Sydney Ferris is seen standing on the right at a presentation lunch held for the staff of Seaton drapers, Ferris & Prescott. The lunch took place in the Bay Hotel in 1964 and Mr Ferris' wife is standing on the left of the picture. The shop in Queen Street traded successfully for over 40 years until Mr Ferris retired in 1974.*

LOCAL CHARACTERS & DIGNITARIES

Standing on the right of this picture is Arthur Stenner who was then chairman of Seaton Urban District Council. He was presenting awards at the Seaton Autumn Show during the mid 1960s. Standing next to him is show secretary, Jim Cross.

George Clare, chairman of Seaton Urban District Council, is accepting a presentation following a Navy visit, c.1972.

LOCAL CHARACTERS & DIGNITARIES

*Derek Good from Beer in his car with the personalised number DOG 2 driving
through the floods in Harbour Road, 1972.*

*Mr George Clare, chairman of Seaton Urban District Council, is pictured here trying his hand at
table tennis with members of Seaton Youth Club, 1973.*

LOCAL CHARACTERS & DIGNITARIES

Above: *Seaton Urban District Council, 20 March 1973.*

Above: *Alan Tawse became the new chairman of the Seaton and District Hotels & Restaurants Association during January 1989. He is seen here on the right of the picture with foreman chairman, Mrs Dorothy Lomas, and hoteliers president, Fred Hocking.*

Right: *Arthur Stringer opens the VJ exhibition in Seaton Museum, 1995. Left to right: Ted Gosling (curator of the museum), Barbara Dearden-Potter (Chairman Seaton Town Council), Roy Chapple (chairman Axe Valley Heritage Association) and Mr A. Stringer a Burma Star veteran.*

ENTERTAINMENT & LEISURE

PRICE 6d.

SEATON AND DISTRICT
HANDICRAFT & HOBBIES
EXHIBITION

of Embroidery, Knitting, Crafts, Carpentry, Models Etc.

(under the Auspices of Seaton Branch British Legion and the Rotary Club of Seaton)
will be held on

SATURDAY, 24th MARCH, 1951.

in the WARNERS HOLIDAY CAMP, SEATON.

PRESIDENT — Vice-Admiral SIR FRANCIS PRIDHAM, K.B.E., C.B.

VICE-PRESIDENTS :

Mrs. A. H. Baylis	Mr. G. W. Hutchings	Mr. J. H. Pope	Mr. F. L. Chard
Mr. G. H. Brewer	Mr. L. J. Lorton	Mr. A. Richards	Mr. T. G. Clapp
Sir Ernest Clark	Mr. H. Darnbrough	Mr. C. G. Miles	Mr. L. R. Miller
Mr. J. H. Mills	Mr. D. H. Morrell	Mr. A. H. Thorne	Capt. H. Warner
Mrs. F. C. Shadrack	Mrs. E. Gladstone	Smith & Sons (Seaton) Ltd.	

Seaton and District Handicraft and Hobbies exhibition held in Warners Holiday Camp, 24 March 1951.

Seaton British Legion dinner, Royal Clarence Hotel, 1951.

Above: *WI Pageant, Seaton Down Hall, 1967.*
Photograph: Byrne-Jones.

Right: *Regal Cinema programme for April 1970.*

THE REGAL CINEMA
Tel. SEATON 260

Programme for April

Axe Vale Amateur Operatic Society. The cast of Iolanthe, *April 1988.*

MIRROR MIRROR ON THE WALL
WHO HAS THE BEST JOB OF ALL?

£18 plus BONUS | FULL Training
40 hr 5 Day Week | FREE Transport

whichever way you look at it
It's a Job worth doing - a Job worth keeping

LADIES, GIRLS, JOIN RACAL, SEATON LTD. NOW!

Harbour Road Seaton Tel: 21100 **RACAL** Ask for Roy Maddocks or David Peat

Advert for Racal, 1972.

Members of Seaton Darby and Joan Club, 1974.

Right: *Seaton Art Exhibition, c.1972*

Below: *Seaton & District League of Friends/Rotary Club of Seaton Summer Fête, Seaton Motel, 1989.*

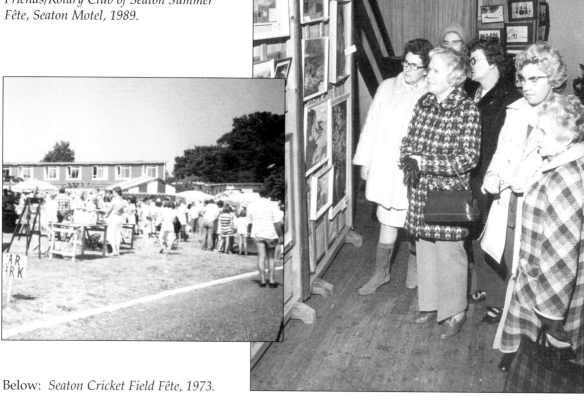

Below: *Seaton Cricket Field Fête, 1973.*

CARNIVALS & SHOWS

Right: *The 1953 Seaton Carnival was organised by the Seaton Football Supporters Club and the Royal British Legion Branch – pictured here in the Town Hall is the local doctor's wife, Mrs Coburn, performing the Carnival Queen crowning ceremony. The Queen that year was Miss Sheila Tolman and her attendants were Miss Josie Hawker standing on the left and Miss Sheila Hutchings. Tragically Sheila Tolman was to die from cancer within a few months.*

Left: *The crowning of the Seaton Carnival Queen in 1951 took place in a marquee on Seaton's cricket field. The Carnival Queen that year was Mary Gooding who is seen here in the marquee followed by her attendant, Barbara Newton.*

Below: *Youth Club tableau in the 1953 carnival, 'Old Uncle Tom Cobbly and All'. Left to right: Brian Baker, Alan Nicholas, Fred Cockram, Stan Pritchard, Tony Combes, David Cockram, Eddie Cockram.*

Above: *Seaton Autumn Show Committee, c.1953.*
This autumn flower show with vegetables was revived by
the Seaton Royal British Legion after the Second World
War. Included are: *Mr Batstone, Capt. Whippell,*
Mrs M. Wolstencroft, Mr H. Baylis, Mr J. Cross,
Mr W. Hutchings, Mr Batstone, Mr A. Gear.

Right: *Muriel Hawker, the 1948 Seaton Carnival Queen,*
makes a silver cup presentation.

Below: *Royal National Lifeboat Institution tableau,*
Seaton Carnival, c.1960. Note the young Tony Burgess
standing on the right. Photograph: Byrne-Jones.

ROYAL NATIONAL LIFEBOAT INSTITUTION

YOUTH CLUB

Youth Club outing, 1952. **Left to right:** *Dick Moore, Don Rodgers, Henry Richard, Fred Cockram, Alan Baker, Buster Way, Arthur Critchard, Gordon Pritchard.*

Seaton boys on a Youth Club outing to Weymouth, 1951. **Left to right:** *Brian Baker, Ted Gosling, Derek Jones, Brian Steele, Fred Cockram, Gordon Pritchard.*

FOOTBALL

Left: *Seaton football team, c.1952. Left to right, back row: Harry Moore, Ron Anning, Bill Keate, Don Rodgers, ?, Alan Baker; front row: Bill Gillard, Horace Critchard, Des Garrett, Len Rodgers, Tony Byrne-Jones.*

Right: *Seaton Football Club, c.1951. Left to right, back row: Bunny White, Alan Baker, Steve Price, Ron Anning, Ken White, Len Pritchard; front row: Ron Nash, Des Garrett, Derek Real Arthur Critchard, Jim Anning.*

Left: *The Seaton Reserves football team who were pictured in May 1953 before a match against Beer Reserves. Left to right, back row: Sam Sluggett, Harry Moore, ?, Gerald Gosling, Len Rogers, Roy Rogers; front row: Des Garrett, C. Hown, W. Anning, Stan Pritchard, ? Newton.*

BOWLS

Seaton Bowling Club team winners with cup, c.1960.
Left to right: *Mr E. Gilbert, ?, Mr Paul, Mr N. Tolman.*

Seaton Bowling Club. This Green was opened in 1929 and prior to that date the game was played on rinks in Colyford Road. Tom Hilder, captain of Seaton Bowling Club, is pictured here throwing up a wood on the opening day of the new season.

GOLF

Seaton Golf Club cup presentation, c.1967. Photograph Byrne-Jones.

Seaton Miniature Golf Links on the Cliff Field, 4 August 1965.

CHANGES FOR BETTER & WORSE

Walt Peach was caught on camera busy demolishing the old shelter on Moridunum, c.1953. Walt is on the roof of the shelter. The young man standing on the right was a member of the Batstone family.

Tree-planting ceremony, Harbour Road, 1954. In 1954 Harbour Road was known as Station Road and in an attempt to make the area more attractive, the Seaton Rotary Club financed the planting of trees. Pictured here, outside the old Geisha Café, are from right to left: Ben Turner, Revd H.R. Cooke, Arthur Thorn planting the tree, Frank Norcombe, Len Chard, ?, Dr Maclean, John Morgan, ?, Charlie Taylor, George Trevett, Dentist Burnside, ?, A.N. Burgess and Miss Archer.

Harepath Road, 1987. The commencement of the Bovis Home Estate helped to destroy an area of outstanding natural beauty.

Seaton Town Council certainly dropped a clanger when they commissioned a Plymouth art student to design a sculpture to stand on Seaton seafront. Following a petition to have the monstrosity removed, the statue was taken down on 22 April 1991 and in the picture, John While, Michael O'Sullivan and Arthur Smith drink a toast as the Seaton sculpture finally left the seafront for a place in some distant theme park. I am told on good authority that this sculpture is now worth much more than the original price.

St Clares

Opening ceremony of St Clares Adult Education Centre, 1 July 1971. Pictured here are the officials at the opening ceremony. Left to right: Mr Eric Jebson (exhibition organiser), Brig. G.L. Lillies (assistant secretary, Music Festival), Mrs C.H. Dixon, Mr C.H. Dixon (who officially opened St Clares), Mr F. Davis (chairman, Seaton Urban District Council), Mrs S. Clapp (chairman of the organising committee), Mrs B. Buckley (committee member), Mr G. Lillies (secretary), Mr W. Buckley (exhibition chairman), Mr A.J. Vickery (St Clares first warden).

Mr J. Morrish on the left of this photograph is showing parents a model of a cardboard tank, a joint production of the pupils' handicraft, St Clares, c.1974

SEATON HOSPITAL

Below: *Seaton Hospital was officially opened on Tuesday 10 May 1988 by HRH the Duchess of Gloucester. Having cost £680,000 huge support from the Hospital's League of Friends over the previous few years secured the town its first ever hospital. Mary Wood (seated centre)* is receiving congratulations for her effort as the leading light in the League of Friends.

Above: *The Duchess of Gloucester officially opened the Seaton Hospital on Tuesday 10 May 1988. She is seen here being greeted by local school-children on her arrival.*

Left: *Local doctor, Bob Jones, at the opening ceremony of the new Seaton Hospital.*

TRAMS

The Seaton Tramway Company originated at the Lancaster Electrical Company of Barnet which manufactured battery electric vehicles. In 1949 the owner, Claude Lane, indulged his hobby by building a miniature 15"-gauge tram which he ran at garden fêtes, etc. This portable system enjoyed temporary homes at St Leonard's (Sussex) and Rhyl (North Wales) before evolving into the 2'-gauge Eastbourne Tramway in 1954. Many of the present trams were built at Eastbourne but by the mid 1960s the tramway's success was outgrowing the two-thirds-of-a-mile line, which in any case was under threat from housing development. Claude Lane therefore began to look for alternative locations. Meanwhile, the Seaton branch railway was under threat of closure. The four-and-a-half-mile line ran from Seaton to Seaton Junction on the Exeter–Waterloo main line. The branch was opened in 1868 by the Seaton & Beer Railway Company, primarily to transport Beer limestone. They sold out to the London & South Western Railway in 1885 which in turn became part of the Southern Railway in 1923. By this time the main cargo was tourists. On nationalisation in 1947, the line passed to British Railways Western Region but car ownership was already causing a decline in passengers. The infamous Beeching Report was the last straw and the line finally closed in 1966. Claude Lane purchased the Seaton to Colyton section in late 1969 and, after a mammoth relocation from Eastbourne, the first section of the 2'9"-gauge Seaton Tramway opened in August 1970. Despite Claude Lane's death in 1971, the tramway continued and the final extension to Colyton was opened in 1980. Seaton Tramway is now one of the area's leading visitor attractions, thanks to the dedication of Claude Lane's successor, Allan Gardner, and his fellow directors, staff and volunteers but chiefly because of the thousands of delighted visitors who make this unique journey each year. In the picture, members of the Axe Vale and District Conservation Society, led by Mr P.R. Noakes OBE, get ready to travel the tramway to view the River Axe and its wading birds, March 1986.

Photograph: Axe Vale and District Conservation Society.

HEAVY WEATHER

A winter's day with snow on Seaton seafront, 1977.

Snow scene, Seaton Hole, 1977.

Storm damage on Seaton seafront, 1977.

Heavy snowfalls in 1977 brought chaos to Seaton. The local council workers were kept busy clearing snow as shown in this photograph taken outside the old bus station in Harbour Road. Photograph: Byrne-Jones.

Above: *Cliff subsidence at Seaton Hole, c.1978. Storms caused a landslide at Seaton Hole resulting in erosion of cliffs in the Old Beer Road with adjacent properties coming under threat. A coast protection scheme to remedy this was commenced in 1998.*

Below: *Seaton sea defences.*

Seaton's sea defences

Seaton will be able to boast a new seafront attraction in the future.

For a new £600,000 sea wall and promenade is being built at the resort by South West Water.

It is part of a scheme to prevent flooding from the sea and from tidal action in the River Axe.

The East Devon resort has a history of flooding. However, floods in February, 1979 were the worst for more than 50 years.

A total of 43 homes and 28 business premises were damaged, together with 240 self-catering chalets and 250 dormer chalets and other buildings at the two holiday camps.

Some properties were flooded to a depth of more than two feet.

 south west water

Constructing the sea wall with steel reinforcements, 10 May 1980.

Constructing the new path to Seaton Hole, c.1980.

Completing the new sea wall and promenade with work at Fishermans Gap, 8 July 1980.

Seaton fishing boat, Gipsy Moth, 22 July 1986.

Storm damage with subsidence on the West Walk, c.1989.
Photograph: Byrne-Jones.

Preparing for the cliff retaining wall by the Castle Hill steps on the West Walk, 13 March 1997.

AROUND THE TOWN

Seaton's distorted circle called The Square, 1961. At that time Boots occupied the corner site next to the George and the chemist shop of Hinton Lakes was in the premises now owned by Byrne-Jones. The Seaton Post Office was then next door to Hinton Lakes.

The River Axe, 1960.

The Old Ferry House, Axmouth Harbour, July 1961.

A summer day in Seaton, 4 August 1961.

Right: *View looking towards the West Walk, August 1961.*

Below: *The East Walk before the sea wall, August 1961.*

Below: *Trevetts Car Park, Harbour Road, 1961. The site is now occupied by Fosseway Court and the Rainbow complex.*

Children's cycling proficiency test, Trevetts Car Park, c.1960. At the time of this picture the Marwyl Café was run by Mr and Mrs W. Woolland. With the Seaton children are PC George Rodd, Ben Turner, Revd George, Mr Shipton and Bob Hoskins.

Looking up Fore Street, August 1962. Note the Golden Lion pub sign in the background on the right. Once one of Seaton's most conspicuous landmarks, the sign with the pub was relegated to history some years ago.

Seaton Warners Holiday Camp in Harbour Road, 1964.

Seaton's paddling pool, 3 August 1965.

Children play in the paddling pool, 5 September 1967.

Roadworks in Fore Street, 1974.

Looking down Fore Street, 1961.

During those post-war years, great social changes took place and much of the old character of Seaton went forever. The major hotels in the resort disappeared and the magnificent Beach Hotel was sold to Devon County Council who, with a taste of what the future held, changed it to an old people's home, renaming the hotel White Cliff. The other splendid-looking Westleigh Hotel on the Seaton front closed, followed by the Royal Clarence and, at a later date, the Bay Hotel. Other smaller premises, including the Golden Lion which catered for the holiday trade, also ceased trading.

After the Second World War, Seaton, like many resorts, enjoyed a boom period, catering for visitors who had not been able to come to the seaside for five years. But the change in holiday fashions brought about by family motoring and holidays abroad, coupled with staff difficulties, led to a severe contraction of the hotel industry in the town. In the halcyon days of the Victorian and Edwardian age the local newspaper had published visitor lists which recorded the names of those staying at the various hotels and boarding-houses. When we study surviving copies of these publications, we realise how much the loss of these hotels and guest-houses damaged the economy of the town.

Seaton has been associated with the Rotary movement since 1948, the local club receiving its charter that year. Since that date it has always been closely allied to the community life of the town and initiated a number of activities whose origin became forgotten as they functioned independently.

By the end of the 1940s, Seaton had a thriving Rotary Club, a local Masonic Lodge, De-La Pole No. 1181, a Lodge of the RAOB Ye Moridunum Lodge No. 5260, a British Legion with over 600 members, football and cricket clubs, two tennis clubs, a golf club and a public miniature golf course, a bowling club and many other organisations catering for all interests.

The Regal Cinema, which opened in 1938, still attracted full houses during the 1950s. It was during this period that, despite local opposition, Sunday cinema was introduced. At a much later date, with falling audiences, due mainly to the new medium of television, it was proposed to close the cinema. This aroused a great deal of opposition in the town and a 'Save the Seaton Cinema' campaign resulted in a petition signed by 2,544 people. Despite all this, the cinema was closed and demolished in 1975, along with the adjoining Violet Terrace. In 2002, this area is the site of the attractive Windsor Gardens, which most certainly presented a vast improvement to this part of the town.

The death of King George VI was followed on 2 June 1953 by the Coronation of Queen Elizabeth II. The people of Seaton once again celebrated with a full day of events, including street parties and sports. The ceremony in Westminster Abbey was seen for the first time on television, that new phenomenon. Local halls installed televisions which enabled people to see the Queen crowned by the Archbishop of Canterbury.

Throughout the 1950s and '60s new housing estates spread out beyond the former boundaries of the town. Development of land around the cricket field, football fields, Harepath Road and Beer Road took place. By the early 1970s, Seaton lost control of most of the town amenities when, following the reorganisation in 1973 of the local authorities, the old Seaton Urban District Council disappeared, with the new East Devon District Council administering the large area of East Devon, comprising differing types of terrain, with villages large and small, towns and resorts.

Seaton Town Hall, the cinema, and the football and cricket pitches passed into the control of this new authority, mainly because the request from Seaton Council to retain these properties arrived too late.

The first meeting of the new Seaton Council was held in September 1973. They were faced with two tricky problems – members did not want to be called a Parish Council and wanted to call themselves a Town Council. Mr Harry Garrod, the clerk of the council, informed them that the regulations stated that a Parish Council could change its name to 'Town Council', but if they did, 'it's chairman shall be entitled to call himself the Town Mayor'. It was agreed that the word 'parish' was out of date. They also felt that the title of Mayor was rather pompous for the duties that faced the new council.

Councillor A.E. Stenner, definitely a wise man, thought that to appoint a Town Mayor was a wrong attempt to gain prestige. Councillor Holland, also a man of much wisdom, thought the phrasing of the regulations seemed to imply that the chairman had the option of calling himself Town Mayor if he wanted to. So he suggested that they have a Town Council but impose a restriction on any future chairman taking on this new title. Recent years saw newcomers to the town reversing this.

The town's new Post Office in Sidmouth Street opened in March 1969. The new modern roomy building meant a new deal for both the public and the Post Office staff, who for years had to put up with cramped conditions. The public enjoyed plenty of floor space and, in addition, first-class facilities were provided for off-duty staff. There was plenty of desk space and an extra partition on the counter provided for extra-busy periods. At the same time, a large room upstairs was fitted with the new automatic telephone exchange equipment ready for Seaton to go on the dial in 1970. The Post Office, with its staff, provided an excellent service for Seaton for over 26 years until, with a backward step, it was moved to much smaller premises.

Seaton suffered a nightmare which began just before daybreak on Tuesday morning, 13 February

1979, when strong winds in the south-western approaches combined with a heavy groundswell to create an abnormally high tide, which advanced across the beach and smashed into the sea-front homes and hotels. The weather conditions that eventually caused the damage at Seaton had built up several days earlier, some 1,500 nautical miles away in the mid-north Atlantic. A depression from this area moved at such speed that it generated high waves of unusually long periods and large wavelengths. These waves swept into the English Channel and coincided with a series of spring tides. A total of 43 homes and 28 business premises were damaged, together with 240 self-catering chalets and 250 dormer chalets at the two holiday camps. Following this flooding, a new £600,000 sea wall and promenade was built at the resort by South West Water.

The value of the constructive use of leisure time by the young people of Seaton was stressed by Mr John Alderson, Chief Constable of Devon and Cornwall, when he formally opened Seaton Youth and Community Jubilee Centre in Harbour Road during October 1979. Mr Eddy Pruden, vice chairman, spoke of the history of the building, sited in the Harbour Road car park, and how it was obtained. It was a proud moment for members of Seaton Rotary Club, particularly Mr Les Warren who had fought for a building to house a Seaton Youth Club since the subject was first broached by Rotarians seven

years earlier. Some 25 years on the Youth Club still provides facilities for the young people of Seaton.

The death was announced in May 1981 of Dr Alex Coburn who, after serving patients in Seaton for 35 years, died at the age of 64. He moved to the district in 1946 and was then assistant to Dr Alan Maclean of Colyton. They became partners when the National Health Service began in 1946. Dr Coburn was born in Aberdeenshire. He was a much-loved and respected man who got involved in many organisations in the town. Dr Arthur Smart was another local doctor who passed away a few years previously. He came to Seaton in 1923 and lived at Netherhayes, Fore Street, where he practised medicine for 27 years before moving to Withylake, Seaton Down Hill, and retiring in 1954.

Today, Seaton continues as a busy thriving town. Over the years it has undergone many changes but it has been able to adapt to the changing requirements without losing too much of its character. Changes of occupation and retirement have brought into the town a large population who were not born there. Although the appearance of Fore Street and Queen Street has not greatly changed, the old names over the shops have disappeared and the Devonshire dialect is seldom heard. Incomers now outnumber the true natives, but hopefully all will help to preserve the rich inheritance that has been handed down through the generations.

The locomotive Seaton was a Light Pacific of the West Country Class No. 21c.120.
The naming ceremony on 25 June 1946 took place at Seaton Junction and was attended
by members of Southern Railway and Seaton Urban District Council.

Chapter 11

ST GREGORY'S CHURCH

It is a little difficult to trace the absolute history of the Parish Church and its architectural growth. St Gregory's appears to have been attached to the Monastery of Horton at first, but by the year 1145 it seems to have passed into the control of the Abbey of Sherborne. Pope Eugenius (1145) and Pope Alexander III (1163) both made mention of Seaton and Beer as being part of the properties of the Abbey of Sherborne. After the Dissolution of the Monastery of Sherborne, Henry VIII gave the manor and church of Seaton to the Queen, Katherine Parr, for life, and sold the reversion to John Frye of Grays Inn. In 1566 John Frye sold it to John Willoughby of Payhembury. In 1655 Sir George Trevelyan married Mary, daughter and heiress of John Willoughby, and thus obtained the manor of Seaton.

St Gregory's Parish Church coach outing c.1930. Revd Robinson is pictured standing in the middle of this photograph.

The church itself is generally supposed to have been dedicated to 'St Gregory', the Bishop of Rome who sent Augustine to our shores in the year 597. However, there appear in ancient documents some indications of the dedication having been that of 'St George'.

It might be safely said that a small cruciform church was probably built in the thirteenth century. The first enlargement seems to have been the addition of the south side chapel in the fourteenth century, probably in about 1350. From some notes which I found in Exeter, it would appear that the church was largely rebuilt in 1360 and a south tower added. This south tower is stated to have been removed in the fifteenth century and the west tower built. Another alteration was the deepening of the north transept to form the Waldron aisle. Subsequent to this, another portion of the north wall was taken down and a further piece of the churchyard enclosed. The last enlargement was in 1817, when the remainder of the north wall was removed, more land taken in and the gallery added.

The choir vestry was added in 1884. An old organ was first in the gallery, then in the Waldron aisle. The new organ was built in 1884. The chancel, judging by a date in the wall, was rebuilt in 1764. The chancel screen, the gift of Revd M.H. Hayman, was erected in 1831 in memory of his wife, Annie Maxwell Hayman.

A general restoration of the church, when practically all the old work was removed, was carried out in 1865. There was at one time a screen, richly decorated with heraldic devices, which enclosed the Waldron aisle. This screen was removed in 1865 and portions of it seem to have travelled far and wide. Many portions, however, were recovered by the late Mr Radford, who at one time lived at Bovey House.

The first record of a vicar of Seaton dates back to 1260. The registers are of interest and date back to 1584. In these registers are many curious entries and many references to the old-time levying of tithes upon fish, orchards, hearths, etc.

In a report upon churches of the deanery dated 1848, it is stated that at that time the joint population of Seaton and Beer was 1,966. The two parishes were divided in 1905.

145

Aerial view of Seaton, 13 October 1972.

Chapter 12

SMALL NOTES FROM SEATON

EXTRACTS FROM THE SEATON MUSEUM NEWSLETTER TO MEMBERS OF
THE AXE VALLEY HERITAGE ASSOCIATION *by Ted Gosling*

Jubilee Clock

Jubilee Clock always held a special place in the hearts of all Seatonians. For over 100 years, standing like a sentinel on Sea Hill, it not only gave them the time, but became the town's most familiar landmark.

Locals returning after a long absence from the town knew they were home when they first caught sight of Jubilee Clock's red-brick tower, and heard that off-key thud when it struck the hour. The clock works were made in Seaton by Mr E.D. Good and, until the 1960s, generations of the Good and Tolman families kept them wound up and maintained.

Following the decision in 1994 to replace the clock works with electricity, the East Devon District Council presented the clock to the Museum, and nothing has given me more pleasure than accepting the works of this old friend for display and preservation for the future.

Benjamin Woodward

Benjamin Woodward is today best remembered as the architect of the Museum building at Trinity College, Dublin, the University Museum at Oxford and the Kildare Street Club, Dublin.

He was born in Tullamore, Ireland, on 16 November 1816, and became a close friend to Sir Walter and Lady Trevelyan. In 1860 he designed the school house at Seaton for the Trevelyans, and in the same year worked for them on a plan for projected terraced houses along the sea front. This project, which he discussed at length in a series of letters to Lady Trevelyan, came to naught. Also in 1860 he designed Calverley Lodge (now Check House, Seaton) for W.C. Trevelyan. The executant architect was Charles Frederick Edwards of Axminster (1837–97), who drew on the designs of Woodward when the house was built in 1864–66.

Although troubled by ill health – he suffered from tuberculosis – Woodward achieved a considerable output, designing over 60 buildings and projects during the last 12 years of his life. He died in May 1861, when staying at a hotel on the Rue de Bourbon in Lyons, after suffering a violent lung haemorrhage. In the late 1860s T.N. Deane, then engaged on the restoration of St Carnice's Cathedral, Kilkenny, had a stained-glass window erected to Woodward's memory in the North Choir aisle. In Seaton we are fortunate that he left his mark with one of the town's most attractive buildings.

Parish Registers

Not many people hold Thomas Cromwell in much esteem but, as the founder of Parish Registers, he can be credited with something wise and good. Parish Registers are wonderfully interesting and informative as to life in ancient times. His scheme was the one commendable action in the public life of this marvellously shrewd but absolutely unscrupulous man.

On 5 September 1538 he, having recently been appointed Vicar General, issued a series of injunctions, including this one:

That you and every person, vicar or curate, shall for every churche kepe one boke or registere where

147

in ye shall write the day and yere of every weddying, christenyng and buryeng made within your parishe for your tyme, and so for every man suceedyng you likewise, and shall insert every persons name that shall be so weddid, christened or buried.

Directions were given for the provision by the parish of 'one sure coffer with two locks and keys in which to keep the book'. Entries were to be made every Sunday, in the presence of at least one warden.

A copy of the earliest Seaton Parish Register is kept in the Museum, and [Ted Gosling] holds the transcript of the Branscombe Parish Registers. From these shortest and simplest of possible annals, the discerning eye can reconstruct something in the life of bygone ages and the rise and decline of villages and towns.

The Parish Registers of Branscombe commence with the baptism of John Duck, son of (unknown Christian names) Duck, 1st October 1539, and John Myco, son of Rainold and Katherine Myco, 1539. During the eighteenth century the local clergymen made useful observations in the Register, and we learn that William Newton, a farmer of the parish, died aged 50 – he married twice, first Rachel Gosling, by whom he had two daughters, and secondly Jane Bartlett, who he left a widow with two children. He died on 29 December 1785, a victim to the horrid sin of drunkenness.

The same vicar, no doubt a pious man, appears to have had troubles with the sinful ways of Branscombe folk. He entered the death of Mary Newton, an 85-year-old widow, on 19 January 1795 with the comment that although she had been kept by the parish for many years, and was to be buried by the parish, she had two sons living in Branscombe who had the means to support her. What is more, she had also been left by her father a considerable sum of money for which no-one can account. Looks like a very early case of Social Security fraud.

Unusual Fruit – The Medlar Tree

My affection for the medlar tree dates back to childhood, when my Sidmouth grandfather had a fine example in his garden. The russet fruits were fascinating, and reminded me of those knobbly objects you see attached to leather thongs on the flail-like hand-weapons of medieval warfare.

When I moved to Quantock over 30 years ago I planted a young medlar with the full knowledge that it would take many years for that tree to attain maturity. It was a tree for those who intended to stay put on their own plot of land, not one for the vagrant tenant.

And 30 years on my medlar, now in full maturity, becomes delightful in May, when it is covered with large white flowers, and even more attractive in the autumn when the leaves turn into a motley of very beautiful variegated colours – pink, yellow, green and brown, freckled with those strange russet fruits.

You should let the medlars hang on the tree as long as possible before you pick them. You can't eat a medlar raw, although they are palatable when they are rotten (bletted is the official term). They taste like a rotten pear covered in sand – I think that is a fair description and, although the Victorians ate them, they are not acceptable to the modem palate.

But they do make a wonderful medlar jelly, an excellent plummy sort of jam which makes a superb accompaniment to roast lamb or venison. My grandson Jorden told me that these clusters of strange fruit look like dogs' bottoms – just think, when I was his age I thought they looked like those knobbly objects you see attached to leather thongs on the flail-like hand weapons of medieval warfare!

Seaton Regatta, Tuesday 27 July 1926

A programme for this regatta was recently passed over to me to add to the Museum archives.

Before the last war Regatta Day was a major event in the Seaton calendar, and was held either on the Bank Holiday Monday or on the previous Thursday. Why it was held on a Tuesday in 1926 is a complete mystery to me.

The programme is full of interest and cost 2d. (old pence). The caption on the cover reads: 'Our true intent is all for your delight'. Now not many of you will know that when Billy Butlin opened his first holiday camp at Skegness, across the front of the main building was a huge illuminated sign which attracted the attention of holiday-makers with those same words. Now you will, of course, know that this is a quote from Shakespeare's A Midsummer Night's Dream. I don't expect Bill Butlin knew this – he had hardly been to school, let alone read plays by Shakespeare – but he had seen this same quote on the front of a fairground organ many years before and had liked it so much that he remembered it and decided to put it on the front of his new holiday camp. Now I digress, so back to the programme.

The sports programme makes interesting reading and commences with the sailing and motor boat matches. The first race of the day was the Brixham Trawlers, and to attract entries to this class the first prize was £12 – a large amount in those days. You may well know that our chairman is a Beer Boy from a Beer fishing family, and one of his favourite quotes is from an old local saying, 'Beer made Brixham and Brixham made the North Sea'. Now this is true, for the first fishermen to trawl from Brixham were men of Beer in their small boats. By the middle of the nineteenth century Brixham's great fleet of over 300 sailing trawlers became one of the finest sights in the South West, and the Brixham men, coupled with the men from Beer, were the finest seamen in the country.

Here again is a mystery – why did they have this event for Brixham Trawlers? Surely, and I am sure that our chairman will agree, the Brixham men would have supported the Beer Regatta, which was to be held during the following week. Was the Seaton Regatta Committee endeavouring to steal a march on Beer by offering such a large prize? Certainly the hard-working Brixham trawlermen could not spend all their time supporting Regattas, it would have been one or t'other, and I suspect Beer would have won.

The Rowing Races commenced at 12 noon and the swimming contests started at 2p.m. The land sports were held in the Cliff Field.

We had a Town Band in those days, and they rendered selections during the day. The day finished with a grand Regatta dance at the Town Hall, which lasted from 9.30p.m. to 2.30a.m. (makes me feel tired just thinking about the time it finished). The advert for the dance states 'dress or flannels', and tickets were 3s.

The Seaton Regatta was then the highlight of the year, the whole town supported the event – Seaton in those days was a tight community, and events like this bound them together. Sadly the Regatta has long gone, but Beer Regatta survives, and Regatta Day is still a significant date in the diary of every Beer boy and girl. During Regatta week the village welcomes back home the emigrants who have settled in other parts of the country, and a great gathering of the clans takes place.

Glorious Seaton

That distinguished author, playwright, critic, Mr St John Ervine, was asked why he lived in Seaton. He replied:

I live in Seaton for several reasons. The first is that its situation is among the most beautiful in England. I do not know any tract of English country so various in its beauty as East Devon, or one where it is still possible for the pedestrian to travel so far without being thrown into a violent agitation by honking horns and wild motor bicyclists. It is a fact, though this may seem incredible to those who live in other parts of the country, that a man may walk for miles through lanes in East Devon which are not infested by speed-maddened people on infernal machines, and that in each of these lanes a variety of lovely sights may be seen. Some of the most beautiful roads I have ever walked are within a radius of four miles of Seaton, and a radius of ten miles includes an exceptional diversity of loveliness. I searched a large part of England before I finally decided to settle in Seaton. In no other place did I discover so much that I wanted.

Another reason I have for living in Seaton is its equable climate. We notoriously have longer spells of sunshine than the vast majority of British towns. I have heard that our fortune in fine weather is a source of bewilderment and envy to the Meteorological Office. King Charles II, in praising the English climate, said that there were more days in the year when one could walk abroad in England than in any other country. This is certainly true of Seaton. I can walk in my garden without an over

Left: *Geoff Marshall is seen here fixing a plaque to a wall in Seaton Museum, 26 October 1987. This plaque commemorates the adoption of HMS Scarborough by the people of Seaton in March 1942. Left to right: Geoff Marshall (the museum's vice chairman), Roy Chapple (chairman), Ted Gosling (curator) and Edna Everitt (secretary to Museum Friends).*

Right: *Miss A. Giles is seen cutting the birthday cake when Seaton Darby and Joan Club held their sixth birthday party in the Town Hall in February 1958.*

Left: *Construction work on the new Axmouth Bridge, 1988.*

Fund-raising in Fore Street for the new Seaton Hospital, 1987.

Every cloud has a silver lining. Seaton Museum's curator welcomes the wet weather in September 1992, which will attract more people to visit the museum following the hot summer.

coat or a hat almost the whole year round. I have noticed that people who go to the Riviera to escape our winter, die there, on arrival, from double pneumonia, whereas the longevity of Seatonians is the despair of the doctors. We think nothing of septuagenarians in Seaton. One has to be well over 90 before a Seatonian will express astonishment at one's age. Centenarians cut no ice in this district. There seems to be one in every family.

We have a lovely river, lovely at ebb and at tide and haunted by every sort of bird. I scarcely know whether I like the Axe more when the tide is in than when it is out. The bed of the river is a rich, red colour that becomes magnificent in sunlight. The long ruffled line of green hills that separate us from Lyme Regis are endlessly attractive and are never the same in appearance two days running. I have been looking at them now for six years, and am still unsatiated by the sight. Our headlands are as various as our inland country. The massive beauty of Beer Head, reaching into the sea like a great bastion; the gleaming chalk of White Cliff; and the multi-colours of Haven Cliff; these make our sea front an unending pleasure to the eye. Add to this, a kindly air that softens the sharpest asperities of the winter, and you will have no difficulty in understanding why I live in Seaton.

Signed: St John Ervine, Seaton Guide, *1935.*

Monmouth Rebellion

The popular uprising in the West Country known as the Monmouth Rebellion must be one of the best-documented of all similar events in English history. This rebellion terminated with the Autumn Assizes on the Western Circuit, which were conducted by the country's most brutal judge, Lord Chief Justice George, Baron Jeffreys of Wem.

Although history reports that Jeffreys, as a criminal judge, was the worst that ever disgraced the bench, we must remember that he had to undertake the wholesale task of trying traitors. The task was so well performed that it made people think before taking part in rebellions again.

We do not hear so much about the judicial brutality of that age, when children were frequently executed for small, childlike offences, and only remember such practices as quartering the bodies of the dead traitors. The age in which Jeffreys lived was brutal and the criminal law even more brutal.

It seems 39 men from Axmouth took part in the rebellion, and over 100 men from Colyton joined them. Only two men from Seaton went, possibly because it was then only a small village, but I like to think that the men of Seaton had more sense than to follow the illegitimate son of Charles II.

Head Family Extracts

All the eight Westcliffe Terrace houses were built by William Head of The Wessiters. When he died, he left the houses to eight members of the family, on condition that they paid his widow £12.10s. per annum until her death, and then they became the sole property of these eight members.

Three of these houses were eventually left to the well-known Mr W.H. Head. One came from his father, William Browne Head, one from his uncle, John Horsford Head, a solicitor in London, and the other was left to him by his cousin, Marion Hole, who died in Middlesex, 28 April 1927.

Mr W.H. Head was born in Vintage House, which later became the town Post Office until it was moved in 1970, and is now occupied by Strictly Business estate agents.

He lived at The Wessiters, which came to him on the death of his great aunt, Sarah Head, in 1895, when he was 21 years old. He was much involved in the local community and was probably the most popular man that Seaton has ever known. A Town Councillor at the age of 21, he was a great sportsman and a gentleman in every sense of the word. An illuminated address was given to him to celebrate his 21 years as Huntsman of the Axe Vale Harriers.

A Letter to Hannah

The letter in verse below, from Joseph Good, reflects the character of a man who was much loved in his native town during his lifetime. The original letter was deposited in the Museum by Mrs V. Webster, his granddaughter.

Joseph Good, born in Seaton in 1795, was a prominent builder, architect and, at one time, banker. He was highly respected and loved for his kindness and quiet helpfulness. He built Check House for Sir Walter Trevelyan and Seaforth Lodge for Lady Ashburton. The Castle and Cliff House (which the family ran as a hotel, and is now known as Washington House) were also designed by him. He lived at The Castle, and his children were born there. One of his sons was Samuel Good, Seaton's first photographer. Joseph owned much of the land around Cliff House, and he gave a strip of it to the town for a roadway – Castle Hill – as a link between the sea front and Beer front. His father and mother were Jacob Good, who died 3 April 1847, aged 78, and Martha, who passed away November 3 1838 aged 71. Joseph Good died in 1875.

It appears from this letter, which was written to his sister Hannah on August 18 1835, that the lodging house business had not attracted many visitors that year (sounds familiar!). One of the two men from Beer who were sent to Exeter gaol may have been Jack Rattenbury's son. Rattenbury was then in his 57th year, and was at the end of an exceptionally chequered career, but his son continued the tradition and was charged at Exeter Assizes during 1835. The new poem by Mr Smith would be the poem entitled 'Seaton Beach' by the Revd J.B. Smith of the Georges Meeting House, Colyton.

Dear Hannah

I long have intended to write,
But for want of a subject, or how to endite
I know not the cause which, but now I have time
And a topic to write on, I write you in rhyme:
When you read my epistle I think you will smile
To think I attempt a practical style.
But I claim not the laurel, my lines too well shew it,
I am not, nor ever shall be a poet:
Well I now can announce that our houses are clear,
And most likely will stay so the rest of the year,
For generally speaking it's been a bad season,
For which (but the times), I can't give any reason,
As the weather's been dry and the heat so intense;
So what's kept them back must have been the expense.
For the most who come here are people in trade,
The beau monde do not, who their fortunes have made.
So if it's convenient and nothing goes wrong,
I shall see you at Seaton, I hope before long.
As many as can make it pleasant to come,
We'll be happy to see for we've plenty of room.
Our anticipation you'll easily guess,
For our friends are all longing to see little Bess;
But as to the spots on her face and her shoulder,
The doctor thinks may disappear when she's older;
As he says, from dentition, they of times proceed,
Which on consideration, is likely indeed.
The next I'll endeavour to tell you the news,
(If aught interesting) your thoughts to amuse;
As you're unacquainted with most people here,
And not knowing much of the people of Beer,
'Twill not wake your father by hearing who's dead,
Who's drown'd, hung, or married, or who's put to bed;
But you'll say it grows irksome, and I had much better
To finish my nonsense, and seal up my letter.

Yet hold for a moment, to tell I won't fail,
Not for their good actions, they have sent two to gaol
But a lack as they term it (and more to their shame),
So they've cag'd them at Exeter, till they get tame.
But stop, there is one thing I must not omit,
As I think it is likely your humour to hit.
I mean the new poem, by Mr Smith wrote,
Which makes our village a place of much note,
And I think you'll be pleased by musing it o'er,
When you find such attractions on this sea-girt shore
Now I told you dear Hannah the whole I've to tell,
And hope you are all, as we all are here, well.
Be now pleased to give my kind love unto Mother,
And also the same to each sister and brother,
Not forgetting yourself; I must surely mind this,
If I didn't you think me most strangely remiss.
To uncles and aunts, and now for the last thing,
Do give my respects too, to Mr James Bastin.
So now my dear Hannah my scrawl I conclude and remain,
Your affectionate brother
J. Good

P.S. My Father and Mother their love also send
To yourself, Mother Sisters and every friend.

A Letter From Elizabeth

This charming letter was written by Joseph Good's daughter Elizabeth Penelope Good to her Aunt Agnes Leatt, who lived at Budleigh Salterton, on May 15 1846. We know little about Elizabeth – she was only 13 years old when she wrote the letter and within a few years was to die at the early age of 24. From the description in her letter of her grandfather's illness, he had obviously suffered a slight stroke. He was Jacob Good, a well-known local smuggler, and the Zeno mentioned was her brother.

From Elizabeth's letter it is possible to get a glimpse of Seaton life through the eyes of a young girl. The new house her father had built would have been Cliff House, later to be Cliff Hotel, and to remain in the hands of the family for nearly 100 years.

She mentions her father's inability to pay for her schooling – he never did and she never went to school – but despite this she wrote beautifully, and was probably taught by her mother.

The original letter, which can be seen in the Museum, was also presented by Mrs Violet Webster.

My dear Aunt Agnes,

When Mother answered your last letter, time would not admit of my writing you, for to write a long letter will take me a fortnight, but now I have given myself the pleasure of writing you a longer letter than I have written you for a twelve month, or two years. We received a letter from Sam on Sunday last, and he informs us that he has paid a visit to you, and also that Sidmouth was likely to be very gay on the 28th, as they are expecting the soldiers there, are any of you going over to see them, I believe Father intends going down.

And to have had the pleasure of hearing my old friend Mr Clark preach at Seaton Church on Sunday last, he came to do duty for Mr Glascott as the Curate was rather poorly, and his subject was upon perfect peace. I think he is altered a great deal since I saw him last, I think he is got stouter.

Aerial view of the River Axe, taken on 13 October 1972.

Right: Julie Rowe (née Payne) participating in the Grizzly, 1998. Recently voted by Britain's leading running magazine as the number-one event in the country, the Grizzly, organised by the Axe Valley Runners, is also classed as the toughest in Europe. Competitors come from all over Great Britain, France, Germany, Holland and even New Zealand to take part in the event, which starts from Seaton Esplanade and attracts over 2,000 runners.

Julie Rowe describes what it feels like to take part: 'Having run both the Grizzly and the London Marathon, I would say they are both physically demanding, but in totally different ways. London just goes on and on, albeit on a flat firm surface, whereas with the Grizzly there is always another gruelling hill, pebbly beach, knee-deep smelly bog or a cliff at Beer or Branscombe. It's a great event and well organised, but not worth taking on unless you train specifically for the Grizzly. Each year the course changes slightly, and it's always more difficult. The course is now in excess of 18 miles and is considered to be one of the UK's toughest off-road races. It is set in beautiful countryside, but when you are so exhausted, the scenery is the last thing on your mind. The only thing you want to see is the Finish.' (Julie Rowe).

Left: Seaton Methodists' new church project site in Scawell Lane, c.1985.

Last Saturday morning Grandfather was took in a sort of paralysis but it only effected his speech he can use all his other limbs only more feeble a great deal. Mackerel fishing is commenced and I hope they will continue pretty brisk and also the lodgers, there are a few familys in, but we have not let our house yet, we are comfortably settled in our new house, and our other is ready for lodgers, and this one soon will.

Zeno is getting on nicely with his writing and chyphering, and when he can write well enough you are to have a note from him. And as to my going to school, Father says I must wait till times are better before I shall have any schooling. Mahala Manly still continues to get worse, she swells a great deal, and they think she will never be better.

How is Mary and Eliza Carter? Please to give my kind love to them.

We are much obliged for your kind invitation but as Father has been so busy in finishing the house we cannot say anything about coming down, and you must not expect us till you see us.

Kind love from all to all, and believe me to remain, your affectionate niece,
E.P.L. Good

Seaton Beach

Infirm, with languid air, that stranger note,
Who leans, fatigued, against yon upturned boat:
A tropic sun has tinged his sallow cheek,
He hither comes departed health to seek,
In India he amass'd an ample store,
But strength declines – he fled the fatal shore,
Physicians pointed out our genial strand,
Seat of the healing powers and zephyrs bland.

Joe Eeles, Seaton fisherman, c.1960.

Henry Clapp

Many of the older members of the Axe Valley Heritage Association will remember Geoff Clapp and the enormous amount of work he carried out for music in East Devon during his lifetime.

A few old Seatonians can still remember Geoff's father, Harry, who died in 1970, aged 90. Harry was a wonderful character, who led a full life involved in the local community. Always interested in running, he won his first race in 1887 running in the jubilee sports which took place in a field which is now the site of the bowling green.

A lifelong music lover, he played the cornet in the old Seaton Town Hall. Before the turn of the present century, Harry, then a young man, helped form the Axe Valley Musical Society, in which he sang as a tenor in the chorus. For over 70 years he was a chorister in St Gregory's Church choir.

During the First World War, Harry served three years in the Veterinary Corps, where he worked with his greatest love, always maintaining that there is something in bestriding a fine horse that makes a man feel more than mortal. Harry loved hunting and was a lifetime member of the Axe Vale Hunt. Old members of the Hunt could recall the times when, as a mere stripling, he first took hounds and how his last season found him with a heart as young and a cheer as shrill as ever.

For six years he served on the Seaton Urban District Council. He was chairman of the local St John Ambulance from its beginning, and their president until his death. Harry was for many years the chairman of the Seaton Chamber of Trade, and he was the oldest member of the police Specials.

In his spare time he helped form the Axe Vale Operatic Society. He was an exhibitor all his life with the Seaton Flower Show and the Colyton Agriculture Society. He was also the driver of the old horse-drawn fire engine.

He still found time to run the Clapps Riding School and here, among the hundreds of people he taught to ride, were the famous music hall stars Gert and Daisy. Harry ran the Clapps Transport business, and I think he was a disappointed man when, after the First World War, Clapps switched from horses to petrol.

During the Second World War he served in the Royal Observer Corps and, until his death, was a very active supporter of the Conservative Party and Primrose League.

In the springtime of his youth he shared the national joy in Queen Victoria's golden and diamond jubilees. In mature manhood he experienced the horrors of the First World War and in old age would have witnessed the great political changes that altered the social status of the country.

Born into a time when the horse ruled supreme, in 1904 he would have seen the first car, belonging to a Mr Diment, appear in Seaton. This was the year compulsory registration of motor vehicles was introduced, and there were only about 8,500 cars in the country.

Harry was a man with a cool mind, well at ease with himself, much thought of, an irreproachable character, gifted, with a wonderful sense of humour.

During his last years he decided to write his memoirs, and they are full of wonderful stories of his youth and old Seaton.

Tales from Old Seaton

Before the turn of the century, an old Branscombe man named Tippy Abbott used to bring over new potatoes and hawk them around the streets in Seaton.

Before he returned home after a hard day, with a full pocket, he would always pay a visit to the Kings Arms. He would leave his cart, which was drawn by a white mule named Jim, outside the pub.

Now one night young Harry Clapp and his friend Bernard Salter, a right pair of mischievous scamps, decided to play a trick on old Tippy and, with great difficulty, quietly took the mule out of the shafts and put him back in the other way about. They then hid to see the result. After a while Tippy, a little worse for wear, emerged from the pub and, getting into his cart, hit the mule with his walking-stick, shouting 'get up there, Jim'. The mule backed the cart into the Kings Arms with a loud crash, bringing the landlord and his regulars outside. With much swearing and some laughter they put Jim back in his right position, and sent Tippy home to Branscombe. As for young Harry and Bernard... well, that's another story.

Akerman ironmongers tableau in Seaton Carnival, 1949.

Severe flooding of the River Axe took place in 1973. The man on the left is Alan White, standing next to his chalet where he had lived for 11 years.

Manor House pupils at music practice, c.1949.

SUBSCRIBERS

Kevin Adams, Seaton, Devon
Frank Akerman, Romsey, Hampshire
Ronald Anning, Seaton, Devon
Albert and Mary Jane Anning, Seaton,
    Devon
James G. Anning, Seaton, Devon
Wallace A. Anning, Seaton, Devon
Patricia M. Bass, Seaton, Devon
Brian G. Bass, Seaton, Devon
Dick and Eileen Bell, Seaton, Devon
Mrs Betty Bendeaux (née Smith),
    Fore Street, Seaton, Devon
Nancy and Bob Benfield, Seaton,
    Devon
Mr Christopher J. Booth
Mrs G. Brazendale (née Crichard),
    Seaton, Devon
Mr and Mrs Alan Browning, Seaton,
    Devon
Karen R. Burges, Seaton, Devon
K.J. Burrow, Bucks Cross, Devon
Jim and Pat Callaghan, Seaton, Devon
Donald Campbell, Combpyne,
    Axminster, Devon
David Carter, Seaton, Devon
E.R. May Clapp, Seaton, Devon
Ann Clare, Seaton, Devon
Mr and Mrs L. Clark, Seaton, Devon
A. Coburn, Seaton, Devon
Vera Coldwell, Seaton, Devon
A.D. and S.M. Collins, Seaton, Devon
Jean Collins, Seaton, Devon
Joyce Colman, Seaton, Devon
Aubrey and Dorothy Cook, Seaton,
    Devon
Alistair M. Cope, Seaton, Devon
Mrs Wendy Crawford, Seaton, Devon
Brian Davies, Seaton, Devon

Gerald W.S. Dew, Seaton, Devon
Andrew J. Dixon, Marlpit Lane
Eleanor L. Duke, Seaton, Devon
Harry Edwards
David Field, Seaton, Devon
Rita E. Field, Seaton, Devon
Nina Filby (née Brewer), Sidmouth,
    Devon
Sally Fitch (née Cheshir), formerly
    of Seaton, Devon
Mr and Mrs David K. Ford, Beer,
    Seaton, Devon
Sybil and Terry Fox, Seaton, Devon
Gordon and Sheila Fraser, Seaton,
    Devon
Ian and Jean Fullerton, Seaton,
    Devon
Revd Norton Giddings, Seaton,
    Devon
Ken and Peggy Goddard, Seaton,
    Devon
G.G. Greenslade, Seaton, Devon
Miss Ellen Gunner, Seaton, Devon
Brenda Hawker, Seaton, Devon
Philip J. Higginson, Seaton Town
    Clerk
Leonard and Brenda Howard
Mr Graham and Mrs Clare Jones,
    Seaton, Devon
The Kerslakes, Harepath Road, Seaton,
    Devon
Mr Derek V. Kitchen, Seaton, Devon
Jane Knivett, Surbiton, Surrey
Norman Lambert, Beer, Devon
Elaine and Gordon Langford, Seaton,
    Devon
Elisabeth S. Laursen, Seaton,
    Devon

Mrs Cynthia J. Lingwood, Seaton, Devon

Walter N. Lippiatt, Seaton, Devon

Margaret E. Little

Eugene and Gloria Littley, Seaton, Devon

Susan J. Littley, Colyton, Devon

Vera D. Lock (née Jones), Seaton, Devon

Moira Madge, Seaton, Devon

Jim and Pauline Marchant, Seaton, Devon

Ann C. McGarrigle, Seaton, Devon

John and June Meakin, Castle Hill, Seaton, Devon

Freda A. Miller (née Stitson)

Gp Capt. H. Mills, Seaton, Devon

Mr Kenneth Mitchell, Seaton, Devon

Keith Nash, Seaton, Devon

William H.W. Newbery, Seaton, Devon

Joan and Ken Newland, Seaton, Devon

Stephen Northcott, Seaton, Devon

Len Northcott, Seaton, Devon

M. Oldfield, Sunnybeach, Devon

Frederick W. Page, Seaton, Devon

Gillian A. Parker, Seaton, Devon

Ray and Marion Peach, Beer, Devon

Dave and Gillian Peach, Beer, Devon

Alan W. Peach (Buddy)

Madeliene Petrie, Blackfield

Andree Pick, Seaton, Devon

Una Porter, Seaton, Devon

Mr and Mrs R.E. Prankard, Seaton, Devon

Pamela Price, Seaton, Devon

Laurence and Valerie Price, Seaton, Devon

Pamela Rice, Seaton, Devon

Roderick Richards, Paignton, Devon

David W. Richards, Newlands Park, Seaton, Devon

Robert and Jo Richards, Ryalls Court, Seaton, Devon

Mrs Kay Rowe, Seaton, Devon

Howard Rowe, Seaton, Devon

Mr John Rowe, Seaton, Devon

Riitta Rowe, Seaton, Devon

Aileen and Peter Runacres, Seaton, Devon

Pam and Dave Russell

Mr and Mrs A.J. Sauze, Seaton, Devon

Mark Shurey

Alan, Eileen and Colette Simmonds, Seaton, Devon

David and Gail Smith, Seaton, Devon

Clifford R. Soane, Seaton, Devon

Joan M. Solman, Seaton, Devon

Franciscan Sisters Stella Maris, Seaton, Devon

S.W. Stevenson, Seaton, Devon

Brian G. Summers, Minstrels, Wessiters

P.J. Sweetman, Seaton, Devon

Mr M.D. and Mrs P.A. Talbot, Whitecliff, Seaton, Devon

Mrs Cherry Tann, Staplehurst, Kent

Christina and Brian Tedds, Seaton, Devon

Barbara and Ray Thompson, Seaton, Devon

Basil and Avis Tompkins, Seaton, Devon

W.J. Turton, Seaton, Devon

Lynda Vanhinsbergh, Seaton, Devon

John F.W. Walling, Newton Abbot, Devon

Arthur H. Way, Seaton, Devon

John Wilkinson, Seaton, Devon

Mary Wood, Seaton, Devon

Mr David A. and Mrs Margaret M. Young, Seaton, Devon

Titles from the Series

The Book of Addiscombe • Various
The Book of Addiscombe, Vol. II • Various
The Book of Bampton • Caroline Seward
The Book of Barnstaple • Avril Stone
Book of Bickington • Stuart Hands
Blandford Forum: A Millennium Portrait • Various
The Book of Bridestowe • R. Cann
The Book of Brixham • Frank Pearce
The Book of Buckland Monachorum & Yelverton • Hemery
The Book of Carshalton • Stella Wilks
The Parish Book of Cerne Abbas • Vale & Vale
The Book of Chagford • Ian Rice
The Book of Chittlehamholt with Warkleigh & Satterleigh • Richard Lethbridge
The Book of Chittlehampton • Various
The Book of Colney Heath • Bryan Lilley
The Book of Constantine • Moore & Trethowan
The Book of Cornwood & Lutton • Various
The Book of Creech St Michael • June Small
The Book of Cullompton • Various
The Book of Dawlish • Frank Pearce
The Book of Dulverton, Brushford, Bury & Exebridge • Various
The Book of Dunster • Hilary Binding
The Ellacombe Book • Sydney R. Langmead
The Book of Exmouth • W.H. Pascoe
The Book of Grampound with Creed • Bane & Oliver
The Book of Hayling Island & Langstone • Rogers
The Book of Helston • Jenkin with Carter
The Book of Hemyock • Clist & Dracott
The Book of Hethersett • Various
The Book of High Bickington • Avril Stone
The Book of Ilsington • Dick Wills
The Book of Lamerton • Ann Cole & Friends
Lanner, A Cornish Mining Parish • Scharron Schwartz & Roger Parker
The Book of Leigh & Bransford • Various
The Book of Litcham with Lexham & Mileham • Various
The Book of Loddiswell • Various
The Book of Lulworth • Rodney Legg
The Book of Lustleigh • Joe Crowdy
The Book of Manaton • Various
The Book of Markyate • Richard Hogg
The Book of Mawnan • Various
The Book of Meavy • Pauline Hemery
The Book of Minehead with Alcombe • Binding & Stevens
The Book of Morchard Bishop • Jeff Kingaby
The Book of Newdigate • John Callcut
The Book of Northlew with Ashbury • Various
The Book of North Newton • Robins & Robins
The Book of North Tawton • Various
The Book of Okehampton • Radford & Radford
The Book of Paignton • Frank Pearce
The Book of Penge, Anerley & Crystal Palace • Various
The Book of Peter Tavy with Cudlipptown • Various
The Book of Pimperne • Jean Coull
The Book of Plymtree • Tony Eames
The Book of Porlock • Denis Corner
Postbridge – The Heart of Dartmoor • Reg Bellamy
The Book of Priddy • Various
The Book of Rattery • Various
The Book of Silverton • Various

The Book of South Molton • Various
The Book of South Stoke • Various
South Tawton & South Zeal with Sticklepath • Radfords
The Book of Sparkwell with Hemerdon & Lee Mill • Pam James
The Book of Staverton • Pete Lavis
The Book of Stithians • Various
The Book of Studland • Rodney Legg
The Book of Swanage • Rodney Legg
The Book of Torbay • Frank Pearce
Uncle Tom Cobley & All: Widecombe-in-the-Moor • Stephen Woods
The Book of Watchet • Compiled by David Banks
The Book of West Huntspill • Various
Widecombe-in-the-Moor • Stephen Woods
The Book of Williton • Michael Williams
Woodbury: The Twentieth Century Revisited • Roger Stokes
The Book of Woolmer Green • Various

Forthcoming

The Book of Bakewell • Various
The Book of Barnstaple, Vol. II • Avril Stone
The Book of Brampford • Various
The Book of Breage & Gurmoe • Stephen Polglase
The Book of the Bedwyns • Various
The Book of Bideford • Peter Christie
The Book of Bridport • Rodney Legg
The Book of Buckfastleigh • Sandra Coleman
The Book of Carharrack • Various
The Book of Castleton • Geoff Hill
The Book of Edale • Gordon Miller
The Book of Kingskerswell • Various
The Book of Lostwithiel • Barbara Frasier
The Book of Lydford • Barbara Weeks
The Book of Lyme Regis • Rodney Legg
The Book of Nether Stowey • Various
The Book of Nynehead • Various
The Book of Princetown • Dr Gardner-Thorpe
The Book of St Day • Various
The Book of Sampford Courtenay with Honeychurch • Stephanie Pouya
The Book of Sculthorpe • Garry Windeler
The Book of Sherborne • Rodney Legg
The Book of Southbourne • Rodney Legg
The Book of Tavistock • Gerry Woodcock
The Book of Thorley • Various
The Book of Tiverton • Mike Sampson
The Book of West Lavington • Various
The Book of Witheridge • Various
The Book of Withycombe • Chris Boyles

For details of any of the above titles or if you are interested in writing your own history, please contact: Commissioning Editor Community Histories, Halsgrove House, Lower Moor Way, Tiverton Business Park, Tiverton, Devon EX16 6SS, England; email: naomic@halsgrove.com

In order to include as many historic photographs as possible in this volume, a printed index is not included. However, the Community History Series is indexed by Genuki. For further information and indexes to volumes in the series, please visit: http://www.cs.ncl.uk/genuki/DEV/indexingproject.html